Letterheads

in the

3rd

#3

Captions
and Design by
Suzanna M.W. Brown

Edited by
David E. Carter

Letterheads

Letterheads in the Third Dimension
First published 1997 by Hearst Books International
1350 Avenue of the Americas
New York, NY 10019

ISBN:0688-15346-1

Distributed in North America by
Watson-Guptill Publications
1515 Broadway
New York, NY 10035
Tel: 800-451-1741
        908-363-4511 in NJ, AK, HI
Fax: 908-363-0338

Distributed throughout the rest of the world by
Hearst Books International
1350 Avenue of the Americas
New York, NY 10019
Tel: 212-261-6770
Fax: 212-261-6795

First published in Germany by:
NIPPAN
Nippon Shuppan Hanbai
Deutschland GmbH
Krefelder Str. 85
D-40549 Düsseldorf
Tel: (0211) 5048089
Fax: (0211) 5049326

ISBN: 3-931884-01-5

SOMOHANO
EDICIONES, S.A. DE C.V.
SOMOHANO EDICIONES Y DISTRIBUCIONES S.A. de C.V.
Tenancingo 9 col. Condesa
México, D.F. -MÉXICO
Tels: 211 7697 / 553 3873 / 286 0726 Fax: (52 5) 212 1581

Once upon a time, designers looked at a sheet of blank paper—sized 8 -1/2" x 11"—and put down words (and maybe some art) on the front and said "this is the letterhead."

Next, they worked on the front of an envelope, and on the front of a business card.

Next thing you know, it became a "stationery set."

But as an interested observer of stationery design, I've noticed an important development: the use of three dimensions in designing business letterheads, envelopes and cards.

More specifically, some innovative designers are using techniques such as:

- printing on the back of stationery items
- using die-cut techniques to create striking images, as well as unusual shapes for stationery pieces
- unusual embossing
- creative foil stamping

...and more.

This book shows some of the best examples of how designers have broken a creative barrier by creating **Letterheads in the Third Dimension**.

technique   *A full bleed photograph of an artifact from the Museum's*
collection is printed on the back of letterheads. Envelopes
use similar photos on the back flap, and business cards
have photos from the collection on the reverse side.

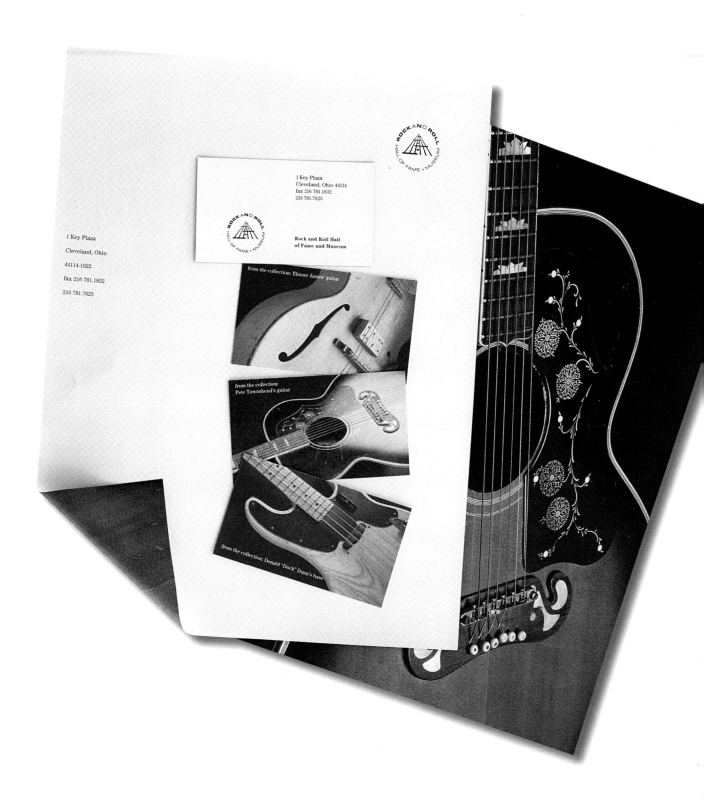

client   Rock and Roll Hall of Fame and Museum
design firm   Nesnadny + Schwartz
                Cleveland + New York + Toronto

From the collection: Keith Moon's platform shoes

6

From the collection: Handsome Dick Manitoba, NYC USA

The Temptations, inducted 1989

technique   *The letters of NAIMA's logo are alternately embossed
and debossed in the upper left corner of both letterheads
and envelopes. The unusual cut on envelope flaps
repeats the curved edge of the printed image.*

client   NAIMA
design firm   Aerial
                San Francisco, California

technique   *Letterheads are sized at 7-1/4" x 10-1/2" and printed full bleed purple on backs. Logos are slightly debossed, printed, and spot varnished on letterheads and envelopes. Business card backs are printed full bleed yellow.*

client   California Center for the Arts
design firm   Mires Design, Inc.
               San Diego, California

technique · · · Blueprints are printed on the back side of this
construction management's letterheads and
business cards.

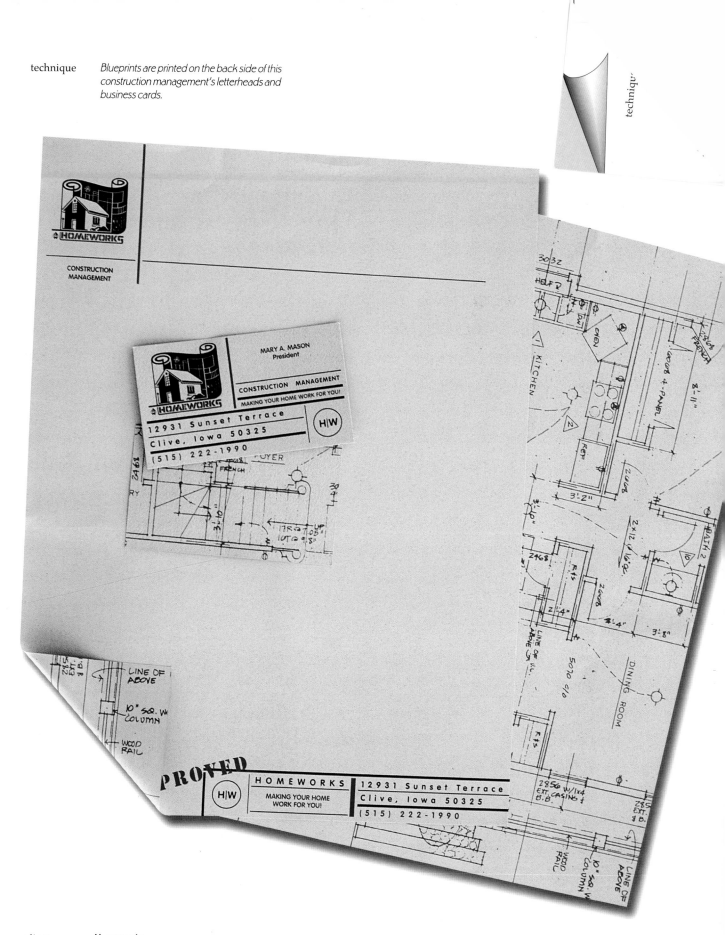

MARY A. MASON
President

CONSTRUCTION MANAGEMENT
MAKING YOUR HOME WORK FOR YOU!

12931 Sunset Terrace
Clive, Iowa 50325
(515) 222-1990

HOMEWORKS

HOMEWORKS   12931 Sunset Terrace
MAKING YOUR HOME   Clive, Iowa 50325
WORK FOR YOU!   (515) 222-1990

client   Homeworks
design firm   Sayles Graphic Design
        Des Moines, Iowa

*This stationery for a fiber artist has variegated metallic
thread actually zigzag-sewn into the letterheads and
business cards. Loose ends were left free to dangle.*

Cranford Creations

Cranford
Creations

YOLANDA CRANFORD
FIBER ARTIST
•
2824 SUMMIT RIDGE
GRAPEVINE, TEXAS 76051
•
817/481-7845

YOLANDA CRANFORD • FIBER ARTIST • 2824 SUMMIT RIDGE • GRAPEVINE, TEXAS 76051 • 817/481-7845

client   Cranford Creations, Yolanda Cranford
design firm   Wet Paper Bag Graphic Design
                      Fort Worth, Texas

14

technique   *White envelopes are centrally embossed at the top and*
             bottom, then printed with white ink and spot varnished.
             The logo is embossed and printed in black ink on one side
             of black business cards, while a name and address is printed
             in silver on the reverse side.

client   **Rees Architecture**
design firm **Muller + Company**
             Kansas City, Missouri

technique   *This design of this stationery package plays strongly on the building theme. It is reinforced by the printing on the back of the letterheads which includes simplified drawings of tools on a wood texture background.*

client   **Equitable of Iowa "Building the Future"**
design firm   **Sayles Graphic Design**
              Des Moines, Iowa

16

technique   *Background printing of a giant wave is continued on all outside surfaces of the envelopes for this dive gear company.*

client   **Tsunami**
design firm   **Mires Design, Inc.**
               San Diego, California

technique   *For Pilot Pictures, a silhouette of a figure holding a toy plane is printed on the back side of legal size paper. Because heavy vellum is used, this printing subtly shows through to the front side. The same process is used for the business cards using only a portion of the silhouette.*

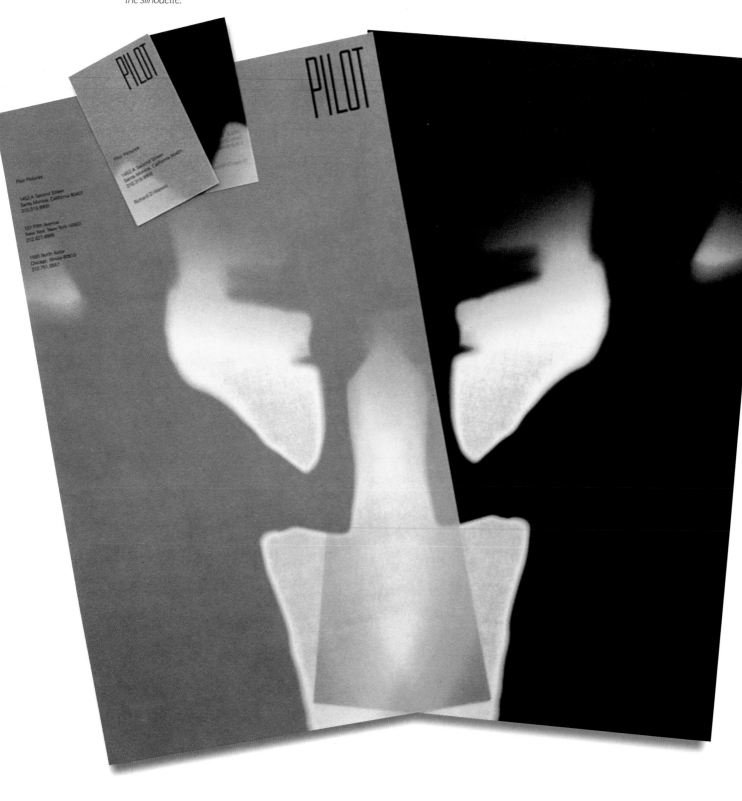

client   **Pilot Pictures**
design firm   **Douglas Oliver Design Office**
                 Santa Monica, California

18

technique	*Unique in size, 3-1/2" x 1-11/16", these business cards are printed with the logo on one side, and name and address on the other.*
client	**Encanto**
design firm	**Boelts Bros. Associates** **Tucson, Arizona**

technique	*Both sides of these business cards use photographs of designers' tools. On the front is the designer's name and street address, with a pen bleeding off the right. Flip it over for the city and phone; the bleed continues from the left as it turns into an artist's brush.*
client	**Dick Lopez**
design firm	**Dick Lopez Design** **New York, New York**

technique   *The reverse of the border texture is printed on backs of both letterheads and business cards. Both backs also carry the company name and product. When folded in thirds, the position of the company name on the letterhead back makes it the first thing one sees when it is pulled from the envelope.*

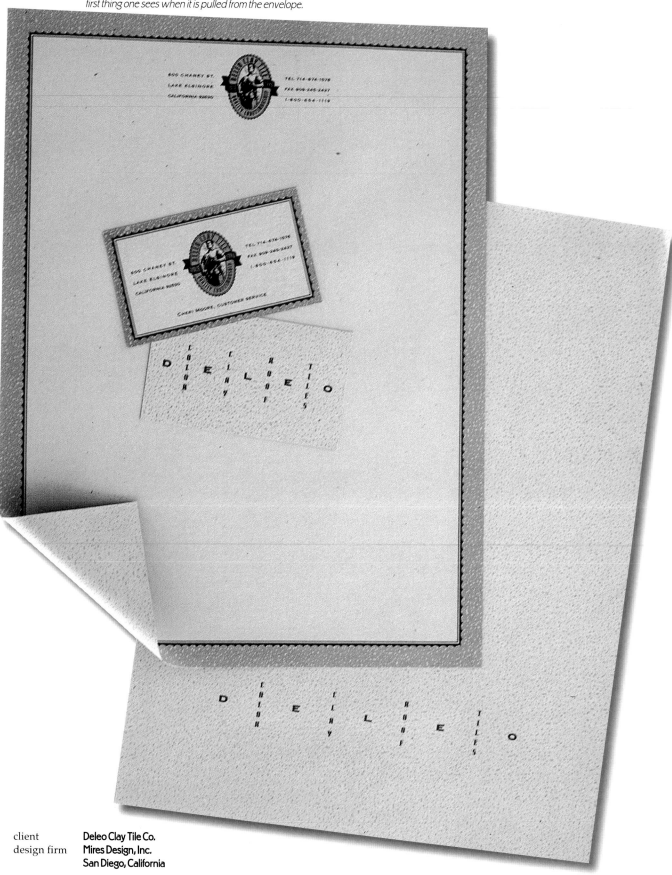

client   Deleo Clay Tile Co.
design firm   Mires Design, Inc.
           San Diego, California

20

technique   *The logo on letterheads, envelopes and*
             business cards is embossed and printed. The
             embossed area on the flip side of the business
             cards is printed with name, title, address...

client   **Nextec Applications**
design firm   **Mires Design, Inc.**
              San Diego, California

21

technique   *The letterheads in this package are die cut horizontally with a "dotted line" 2/3 of the way down the page— easy folding, and/or easy removal and return. Business cards feature a full bleed printing with a statement of ownership in reverse.*

client   The Design Foundry
design firm   The Design Foundry
                Madison, Wisconsin

22

technique   *The company's logo is singly featured on the front of each stationery piece, in reverse on the business cards. Name and address are found on each piece on opposite side to the logo. Strong colors are printed on the back of letterheads, inside of envelopes, and front of business cards.*

client   **The Second Opinion**
design firm   **After Hours Creative**
                Phoenix, Arizona

23

technique   *After printing, each piece is hand stamped with address and phone—address on back of business cards. Letterheads are pop riveted with a hand stamped tag listing the services this firm offers. Envelopes have informational stickers on the bottom right corner. A sequin star is glued in the bottom right corner of the business cards, while a name from a label maker is stuck on the left side.*

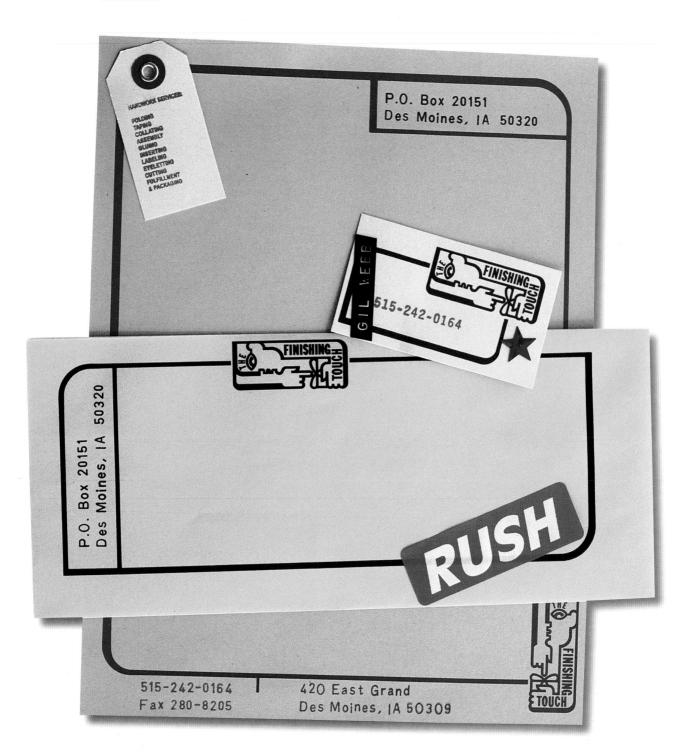

client   The Finishing Touch
design firm   Sayles Graphic Design
                   Des Moines, Iowa

24

technique   *The company's name inside the logo is debossed and gold foil stamped. Letterheads and business cards have the interior image of the logo embossed and printed.*

client   **Fisher Management Company**
design firm **Dean Design/Marketing Group, Inc.**
             Lancaster, Pennsylvania

technique   *The firm's name is printed backwards on the back side of the*
letterheads. Visible from the front, this leaves the impression of a
watermark. Logoesque stripes are printed on both sides of
envelopes. An additional vellum sheet, which can be used with
any of Aerial's correspondence, is lightly printed with the logo in
reverse.

client	Aerial
design firm	Aerial
	San Francisco, California

technique   *The logo is embossed and printed on letterheads, envelopes, and business cards. The logo is additionally printed on the back of the business cards; the address in reverse. Envelope insides are printed with the company's signature bright yellow.*

client   Muller + Company
design firm   Muller + Company
              Kansas City, Missouri

28

Using only black ink, a pattern of bold wedding images is printed on the back of letterheads and inside of envelopes. Visible from the front of each piece, this gives a textured effect. Business cards are also printed on both sides. One side of business cards includes the logo and address, the other has the business name, individual's name, and either a groom or bride, depending on the sex of the card owner.

client   Schaffer's Bridal Shop
design firm   Sayles Graphic Design
              Des Moines, Iowa

Two sets of stationery were chosen by this company.
The design is the same, but the logo is printed in
nonmetallic gold on one and green on the other.
Business card backs include a full bleed of either
color with pertinent information in reverse.

client   **Williamson Landscape Architecture**
design firm   **Michael Courtney Design**
                Seattle, Washington

30

technique   *Envelope flaps and business card backs are printed*
with logo and address. The company's name is
printed on the front side of these pieces. A copper-
colored, metallic ink is used to print the logo and name
on letterheads, envelopes, and business cards.

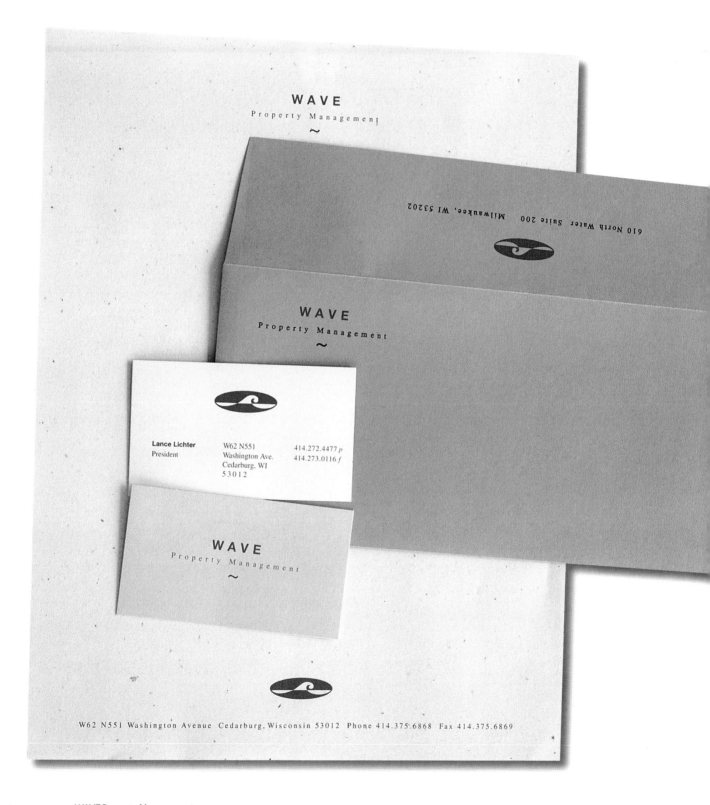

client   **WAVE Property Management**
design firm   **Becker Design**
              Milwaukee, Wisconsin

technique   *Logo and address are printed in black and silver on front of letterheads and envelopes. The logo is embossed. On back of letterheads and inside of envelopes, a full bleed is used to print the blurred image of a bird in flight.*

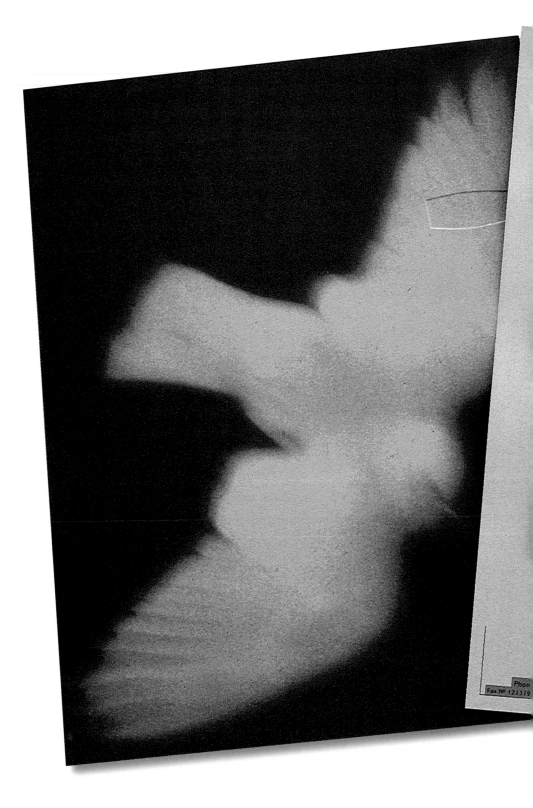

Phon
Fax Nº 121319

client   BRD Design
design firm   BRD Design
              Hollywood, California

technique   *A muted splatter texture is printed on the backs of*
letterheads and business cards. Business card backs
also carry several dictionary definitions of "idiom".
Envelope flaps, in dictionary-definition form, are printed
with name address, phone, and fax.

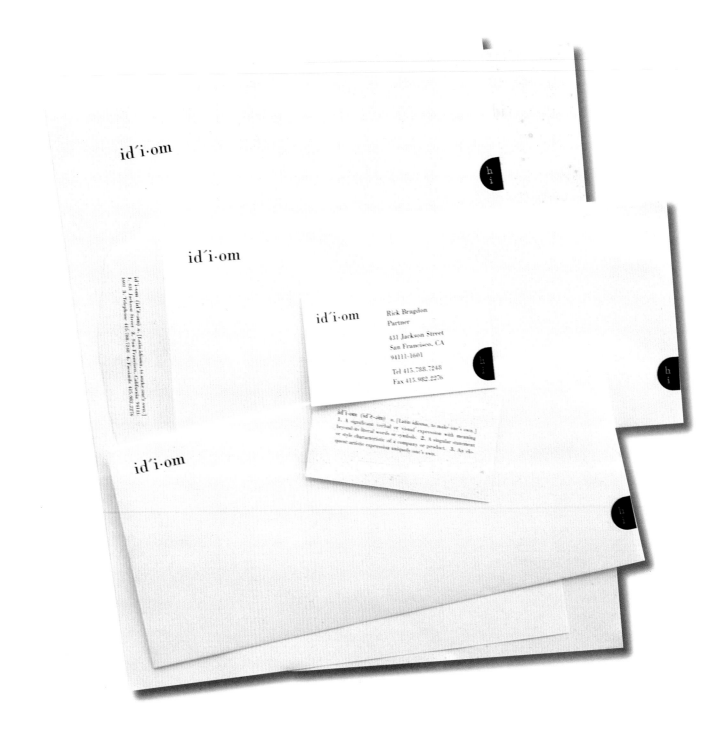

client   **Idiom**
design firm   **Aerial**
                 San Francisco, California

34

technique   *Mushrooms from the logo were used to make a pattern,*
             then printed in a muted shade on the back of letterheads
             and inside of envelopes.

client   Creekside Mushrooms Ltd.
design firm   A - Z Communications, Inc.
              Pittsburgh, Pennsylvania

technique   *Envelope insides, and letterhead and business card backs were all printed full bleed, each with a different color from the logo.*

client   Dimensional Impressions
design firm   McNulty & Co.
                   Thousand Oaks, California

technique   *Backs of letterheads, business cards, envelope insides*
are printed full with a deep blue ink. Envelope flaps have
the logo and tag line. Business card backs include the
logo printed in a bright green.

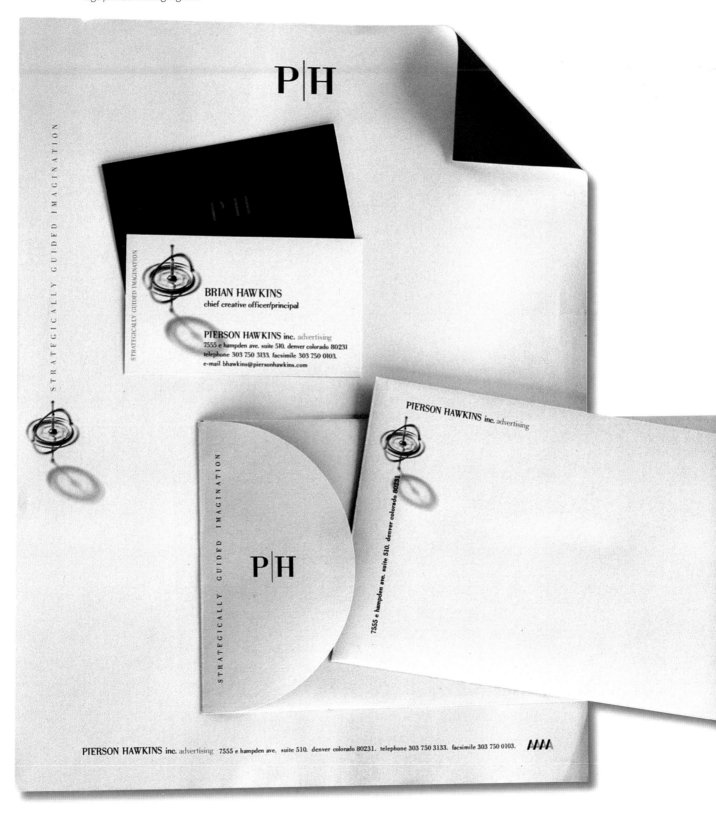

client   **Pierson Hawkins, Inc.**
design firm   **Pierson Hawkins, Inc.**
              Denver, Colorado

technique   *Bright green is printed full bleed on backs of both the letterheads and business cards. A collage with an interntional/informational/financial theme is also printed on that side.*

client   GoodNet
design firm   After Hours Creative
              Phoenix, Arizona

E-Mail: info@goodnet.com
404 South Mill, Ste.C201
Tempe, Arizona 85281
Fax: 602.303.0550
Tel: 602.303.9500

E-Mail: info@goodnet.com
404 South Mill, Ste.C201
Tempe, Arizona 85281

technique   *Simple but effective, the logo on letterheads, envelopes,*
and business cards is embossed and printed.

client   **Kapstone**
design firm   **Muller + Company**
          Kansas City, Missouri

40

technique   *McNulty & Co.'s logo is printed on the top third of the backside of the letterhead so that when the sheet is folded and removed from an envelope, the logo is the first thing seen. Business cards are 7" x 2", die cut and folded so the cut exposes the logo, which is printed on the inside along with remaining information.*

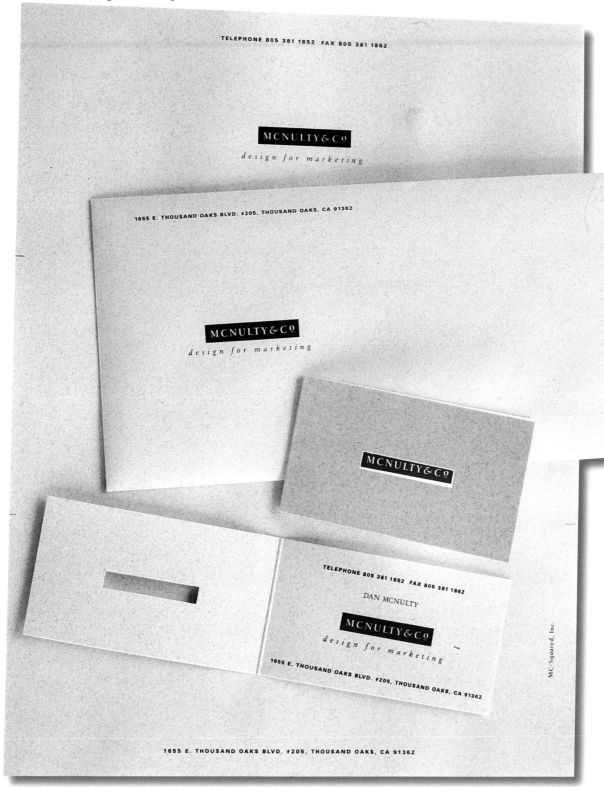

client   McNulty & Co.
design firm   McNulty & Co.
     Thousand Oaks, California

technique   *A bold statement is made with full bleed printing of solid color. The backs of letterheads and business cards use navy blue. Envelopes of one size are printed with plum, another size utilizes forest green.*

client   **Douglas Oliver Design Office**
design firm   **Douglas Oliver Design Office**
               Santa Monica, California

42

technique   *Not only is the front of letterheads printed with the logo and mechanic's tools, the back has a large screen of the sam* *Envelopes are printed front and back with tool images. Perhaps most effective, one side of business cards is printed with a three-sided bleed and logo. The other side carries address, phone, and fax printed on a screened tire track.*

client   **Beckley Imports**
design firm   **Sayles Graphic Design**
              Des Moines, Iowa

An antique map printed in bright yellow is a unifying theme of this package. Used as a border on the front side of letterheads, it is printed with a three-sided bleed on the back excluding only the area on which it is printed on the front. Envelopes have the same map printed inside.

client   Disegno
design firm   Disegno
                Macungie, Pennsylvania

technique   *Logos on all pieces of stationery are embossed and printed. Legal size letterheads are printed at the top with one of four primary color bars which has a spatter texture. The back of each sheet and business card is printed with a full bleed of the same spattered color.*

client   JDO+Associates
design firm   Douglas Oliver Design Office
                Santa Monica, California

46

technique   *Fire engine red and bright yellow are eye catching colors in this package. Letterheads, envelopes, and business cards all have an angled, red and white striped border. Red is printed full bleed on the letterhead backs. Envelope flaps are yellow; insides are red; backs are red with the striped border. Business card backs are printed full bleed red with a message or special offer in reverse.*

client   Chicago Dog and Deli
design firm   Sayles Graphic Design
             Des Moines, Iowa

technique   *Letterheads are an unusual size, 7-5/8" x 11". A slit near the upper right corner facilitates folding down that corner on which the name and address are printed. Business cards are 3" x 1-1/4".*

client   **DFacto**
design firm   **DFacto**
           Balboa, California

DFacto
714 675 9600
fax/modem 675 9900
1544 Miramar Drive #3
Balboa CA 92661

DFacto   1544 Miramar Drive #3
Balboa CA 92661

Mike Ousley

DFacto   714 675 9600
fax/modem 675 9900
1544 Miramar Drive #3
Balboa CA 92661

technique   *This association's architectural logo is blind embossed*
                  on stationery pieces.

NORTHWESTERN ATRIUM CENTER
merchants association

NORTHWESTERN ATRIUM CENTER
merchants association

500 West Madison Street • Chicago, Illinois 60661-2590

NORTHWESTERN ATRIUM CENTER
merchants association

500 West Madison Street • Suite 300 • Chicago, Illinois 60661-2590

500 West Madison Street • Suite 300 • Chicago, Illinois 60661-2590 • (312) 466-7000 • Fax (312) 466-7159

client   **Tishman Midwest**
design firm   **McKnight Kurland Design**
              Chicago, Illinois

technique   *Elements from a blueprint are printed on letterheads,
envelopes, and business cards. Business cards have an
appropriate quote from Winston Churchill on the back.*

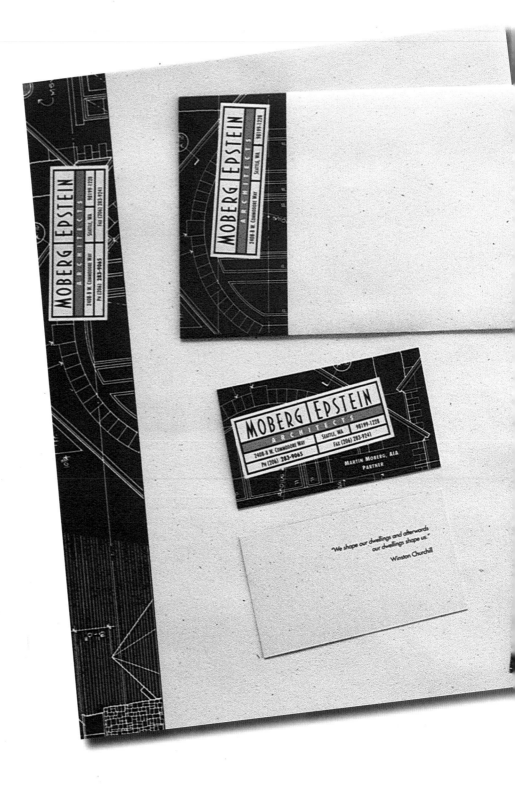

client   Moberg Epstein Architects
design firm Michael Courtney Design
            Seattle, Washington

technique   *Dotted lines are printed on letterheads offering a place to write. The*
reverse side of letterheads have the circle-and-S logo printed in fine
lines. There is a vinyl band which can be slid around the papers when
they are folded. The same lined logo is printed on the band, and when
it aligns with the logo on the sheet a nice shadow or moiré effect is
created. Business cards are three part. Inside the 3-1/2" x 2" vinyl
band, which is printed full bleed with the lined logo, is a white card
with the same printing. When that card is removed, another card
which is glued inside the band is visible. This one is printed with
a solid "S" with the address and phone in a circle.

client   **Sagmeister Inc.**
design firm **Sagmeister Inc.**
             New York, New York

technique   *The Media logo is blind embossed in the same size on letterheads, envelopes, and business cards. It is placed horizontally on letterheads and business cards, vertically on envelopes.*

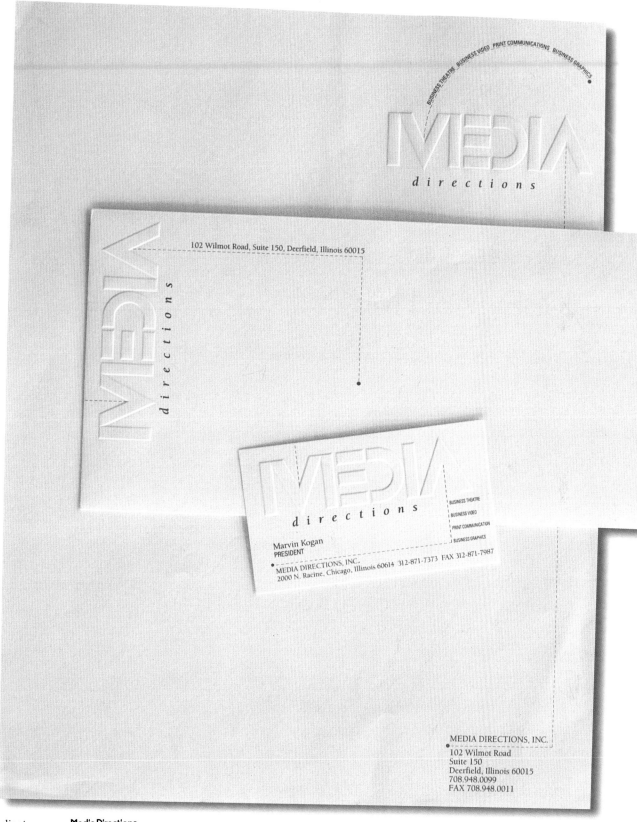

client   **Media Directions**
design firm   **McKnight Kurland Design**
                Chicago, Illinois

technique   *Letterhead backs are printed full bleed with one ink.*
Images of woodcut style graphics and livestock
photographs reminiscent of the 1920s or 30s are used
on a strong grid layout. Business cards also use a grid
format but the back is nearly all text reversed from a one-
color full bleed.

client   801 Steak & Chop House
design firm   Sayles Graphic Design
              Des Moines, Iowa

54

technique   *A marble texture is printed full bleed on the back of*
letterheads. The same marbling is printed in a different
color on the inside of envelopes.

client   **Rosewater Construction**
design firm   **Unit One, Inc.**
               Denver, Colorado

technique   *Mimicking the top edge of a brown paper bag, a wavy edge is die cut on this lunch service's letterheads and business cards.*

client   Barb's Brown Bag
design firm   Denise Kemper Design
              Wadsworth, Ohio

technique   *Stickers printed with the logo are attached to letterheads, envelopes, and business cards. Besides adding dimensionality to the stationery, there's only one printing with an extra color charge.*

46
North
Los
Robles
Avenue

Pasadena
California
91101

818
577
8120

46
North
Los
Robles
Avenue

Pasadena
California
91101

client   **Asian Art Restoration**
design firm   **Julia Tam Design**
              Palo Verdes, California

technique   *One of three very different illustrations, all suggesting*
spatial relationships with regard to interior design, is used
on letterheads, envelopes, and business cards. Business
cards can be turned over for name and address.

client   Jalbert, Rasnack, Anglin
design firm   Michael Courtney Design
              Seattle, Washington

technique   *Printed on both sides with threads attached to either end, these business cards are a game with instructions. "If you spin the card and watch from afar, you'll see the chicken sit on the jar."*

client   **Little Gold**
design firm   **Sagmeister**
                    New York, New York

60

technique   *Select logo elements are embossed and printed, giving a*
real feeling of depth to the dimensional logo.

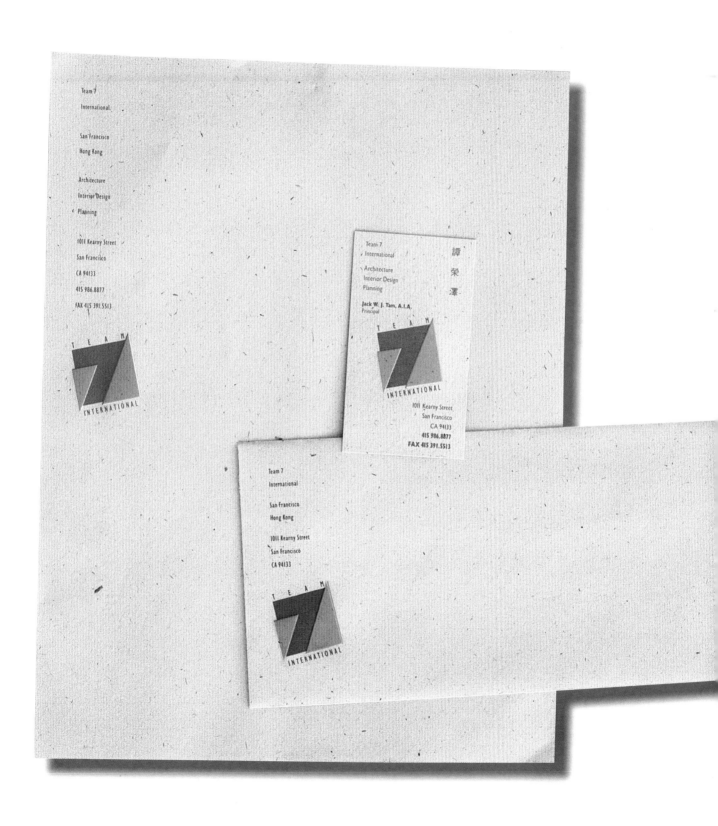

client   **Team 7 International**
design firm   **Julia Tam Design**
              Palos Verdes, California

technique	*Letterheads and business cards are blind embossed and debossed. Debossing the logo background gives the raised logo an even higher and more distinct feel.*
client	**Julia Tam Design**
design firm	**Julia Tam Design**
	Palo Verdes, California

technique	*A very dark, very subtly textured background is printed full bleed on the back of letterheads, business cards, and inside envelopes. An almost scribbled initial logo is reversed from this on letterhead backs and can be seen from the front as a watermark. Name and address are reversed from the texture on business card backs.*
client	**Michael Doss**
design firm	**Hornall Anderson Design Works**
	Seattle, Washington

63

technique   *All paper used is a stock that includes fine gray pinstripes. One logo element is embossed and foil stamped with blue on letterheads and envelopes. On business cards it is foil stamped only. The backs of letterheads and envelope insides are printed full bleed bright yellow. Two types of business cards are printed. On one side they are printed full bleed yellow and have foil stamped logo. On the inside of the folded cards, or the flip side of the traditional ones, is name, address, and numbers.*

client   MMG Worldwide
design firm   MMG Worldwide
               Kansas City, Missouri

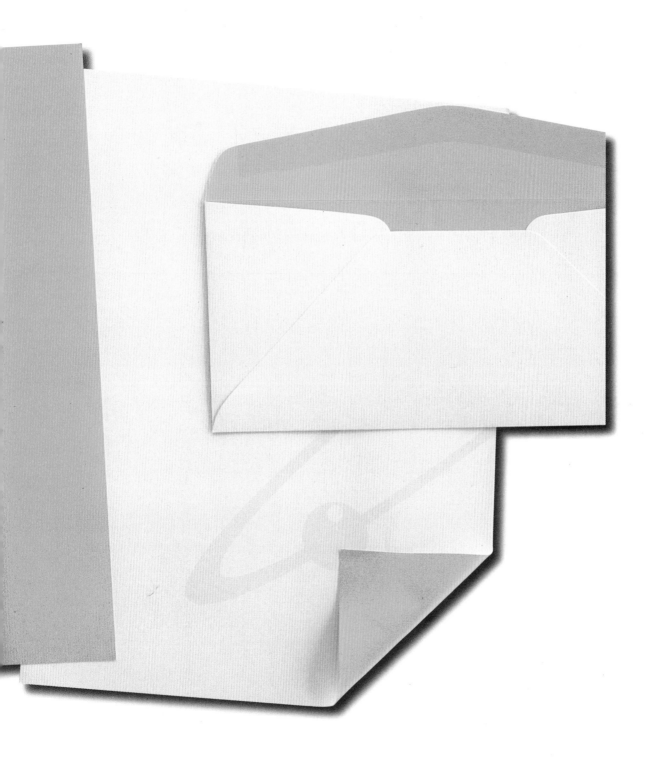

technique *Printed full bleed on the back, letterheads and business cards include either sporting or celebratory imagery. The bullet in the company's name is a small die cut circle on the front, but on letterhead backs the circle is the hole on a putting green. On business card backs it is either the mouth on a bottle of champagne, or the pin hole for an air valve on a basketball.*

client   **Dyce Friend Promotions**
design firm   **Greg Welsh Design**
             Seattle, Washington

Using four different color schemes, this package is an eye catcher. Letterheads are printed full bleed on the back with a large screened logo. Envelopes are printed full bleed on the inside with a solid color. Business cards have company's and individual's name with mailing address and phone numbers on one side. The backs are printed with the street address and Internet site.

client   Quebecor Integrated Media
design firm Hornall Anderson Design Works
            Seattle, Washington

technique   *With the small red square logo, a warm gray is printed*
             full bleed on letterhead and business card backs, and
             envelope insides. The square is debossed on
             letterheads and envelopes.

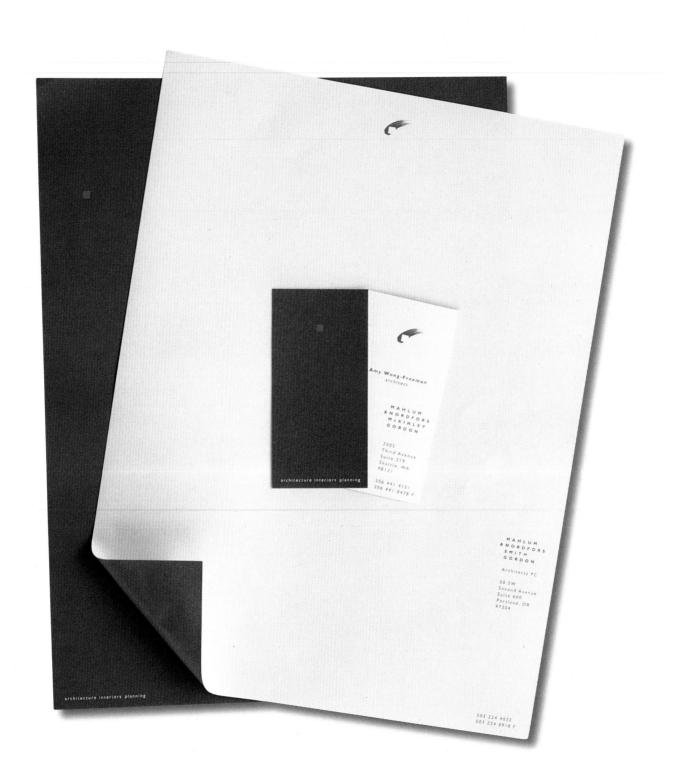

client   Mahlum & Nordfors McKinley Gordon
design firm Hornall Anderson Design Works
             Seattle, Washington

68

technique   *Envelope flaps and business card backs are printed full
bleed black with the logo reversed out.*

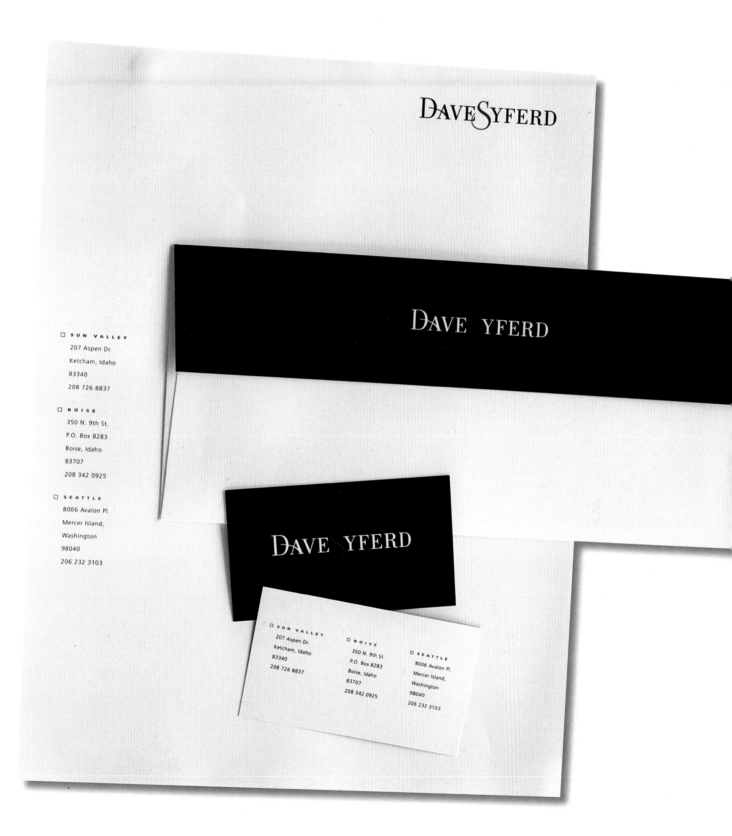

client   **Dave Syferd**
design firm   **Hornall Anderson Design Works**
                Seattle, Washington

technique   *Paper chosen for letterheads and envelopes has a very*
                 subtle texture with a basket-weave watermark effect.
                 Slightly different images of folded paper are printed full
                 bleed in khaki on the backs of letterheads, business
                 cards, and envelope flaps. The front of stationery pieces
                 has one of the logo elements blind embossed. Business
                 cards are atypically sized at 3-5/8" x 1-11/16".

70

client   Greg Welsh Design
design firm   Greg Welsh Design
                    Seattle, Washington

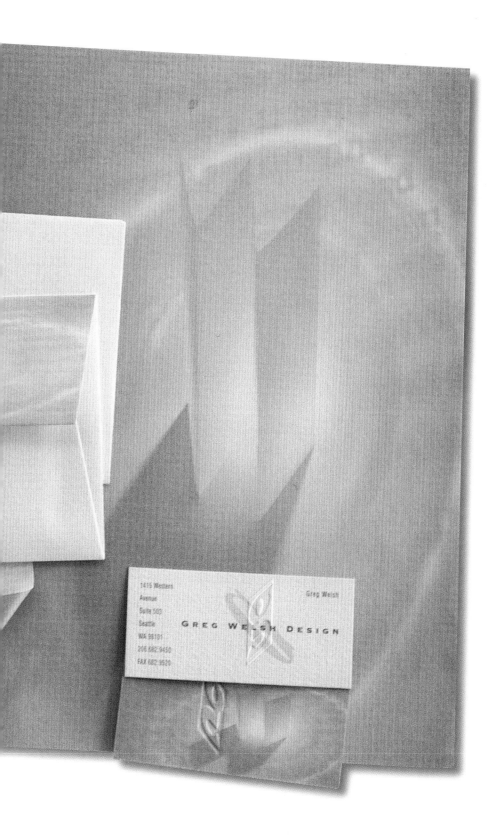

technique   *Monochromatic photographs of architectural elements of the Des Moines Art Center are printed in a collage on the back of letterheads. Vellum envelopes provide visual interest when letterheads are folded and placed inside them. The top half of a label highlighting Auction '96 is glued to the envelope flaps. Just peel the back off the bottom half of the label and stick.*

client	Des Moines Art Center
design firm	Sayles Graphic Design
	Des Moines, Iowa

72

technique   *A textured stock is employed in this stationery package.
Two levels of embossing add to the logo's effectiveness.
Logo background is embossed with a noticeable texture
while the dominant element is raised higher than the
rest.*

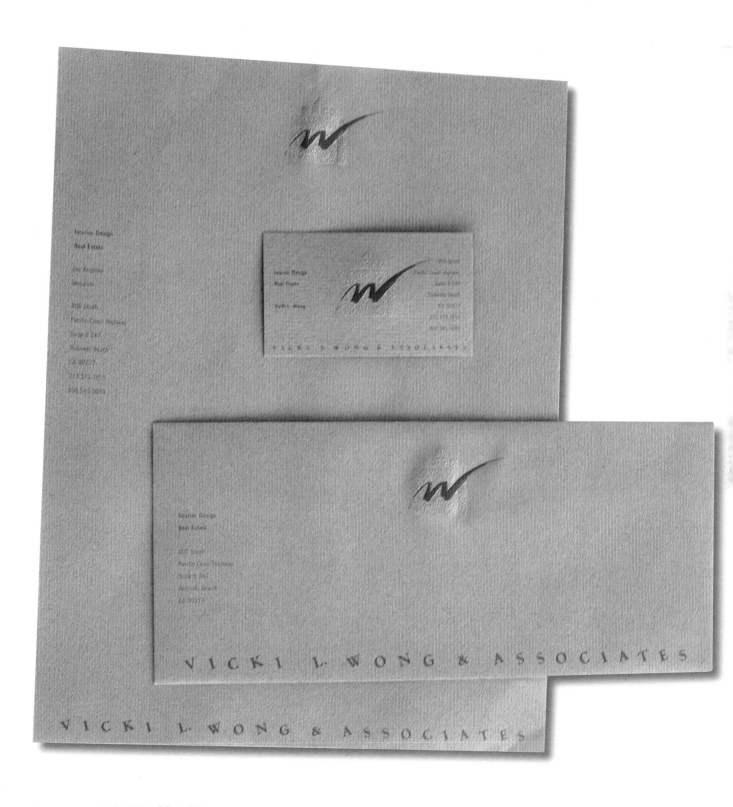

client   **Vicki L. Wong & Associates**
design firm   **Julia Tam Design**
               Palos Verdes, California

technique *The hilltop curve from the logo is repeated at the top of letterheads with the aid of die cutting. Envelope fronts and backs are printed with an enlarged, muted, partial version of the logo. As on the top of letterheads, envelope flaps display the full logo which utilizes copper foil stamping.*

Suite 1029 Two Ruan Center
Des Moines Iowa 50309

Suite 1029 Two Ruan Center
Des Moines Iowa 50309
515.245.3897 • Fax 245.5462

client   **Hillside Neighborhood**
design firm   **Sayles Graphic Design**
                Des Moines, Iowa

74

technique   *Letterhead backs are printed full bleed with a solid warm pink.*

The
Fertility
@Hormone
Center
OF MONTEFIORE MEDICAL CENTER

ive. Dobbs Ferry, New York 10522   Telephone (914) 693-8820   Fax (914) 693-5428

client   **The Fertility & Hormone Center**
design firm   **Mike Quon Design Office, Inc.**
                New York, New York

technique   *Strong colors and often primal graphics make this stationery stand out. One side of business cards offers business, name, address, and numbers. The other is printed with a three-sided bleed of bright color with a reversed graphic image. Information-wise, one finds an individual's name and business number.*

client   **Boelts Bros. Associates**
design firm **Boelts Bros. Associates**
    Tucson, Arizona

technique   *A photographer's stationery, letterhead backs are printed full bleed with full color photos—different subjects, somewhat similar style. Vellum envelopes allow pictures to pique the recipient's interest before correspondence is opened.*

client   **Scott Morgan Photography**
design firm **Lisa Levin Design**
     Mill Valley, California

78

technique   *Royal blue with logo is printed full bleed on envelope flaps and business card backs. Company name and address is reversed from this.*

client   **Alta Beverage Company**
design firm   **Hornall Anderson Design Works**
               Seattle, Washington

technique   *Shadowy deep gold is printed full bleed on the back of*
business cards, as is a black "X" element from the logo.

client   **NEXTLINK Corporation**
design firm   **Hornall Anderson Design Works**
Seattle, Washington

technique   *Laminated business cards are sure to last. Corners are*
rounded. Back is printed with badminton players. Fronts
of cards are printed with a badminton court on which
the players appear when the card is lighted from behind.

client   **Armin Schneider**
design firm   **Sagmeister Inc.**
New York, New York

technique   *A cyan and magenta "floor mat" texture is printed full bleed on the back of letterheads and business cards. The logo, in partial form, is incorporated into this effect.*

client   Sbemco International
design firm   Sayles Graphic Design
              Des Moines, Iowa

technique   *Beautiful fantasy artwork is printed full bleed inside*
envelopes and on the back of business cards.
Envelopes are printed front and back with a
honeycomb texture. Envelope flaps are printed full bleed
black with illustrative logo, and name and address
reversed.

client   Wild Honey, a division of Ottenheimer Publishers, Inc.
design firm   Bea Jackson
              New York, New York

technique   *Part of a large red and white bull's-eye is printed full*
bleed on letterhead backs, and the front side of
envelope insides. Red printing shows through to the
front side for a more subtle version of the same image.

client   Acumen Group
design firm   Sayles Graphic Design
                  Des Moines, Iowa

84

technique   *Crayoned images reverse out of full bleed red on the*
             back of letterheads. Images are drawn in a rough grid
             layout.

client   **American Heart Association**
design firm   **Sayles Graphic Design**
              Des Moines, Iowa

technique   *A pattern in the style of the logo is printed full bleed in*
              maroon on letterhead backs.

client   **Andy and Teri TeBockhorst**
design firm   **Sayles Graphic Design**
                Des Moines, Iowa

technique   *Curved corners and unusual angles copied from the company's logo give this stationery package its uniqueness. Bottoms of letterheads, envelope flaps, and business cards are all narrower than top edges; right sides are longer than lefts. Fabric swatches are printed two-sided bleed on letterhead and envelope backs. Business card backs are printed full bleed with a screened fabric swatch and overprinted with address and phone numbers. The logo is embossed and printed on all pieces.*

client   I.A. Bedford
design firm   Sayles Graphic Design
              Des Moines, Iowa

technique   *A pattern developed from the letters and number in the logo is printed full bleed on the backs of letterheads and business cards, and inside envelopes. Each partner in this firm has his initial as the dominant element on the back of his business card.*

client   Cf2GS
design firm   Hornall Anderson Design Works
                Seattle, Washington

technique   *Simple but distinctive, the upper right corners of*
letterheads and business cards are curve cut to echo
one of the logo shapes. Business cards are printed full
bleed yellow on the back.

client   **The Distribution Network**
design firm   **Sullivan Pattison Clevenger**
Portland, Oregon

90

technique   *Using colors that demand attention, letterhead fronts are printed full bleed nonmetallic gold. Backs are printed full bleed red. Envelope fronts and backs are printed the same red with the exception of envelope flaps. These are full bleed black with the address in white and red. Business card fronts and backs are also full bleed black; name and logo on fronts, address and numbers on backs. The logo, which is printed on each piece, includes, nonmetallic gold, white, red and black. The black portion is slightly debossed and spot varnished.*

client   Sayles Graphic Design
design firm   Sayles Graphic Design
Des Moines, Iowa

technique   *Very nicely done, the address section of letterheads is defined by a blind embossed line that runs from top to bottom edge. At the bottom and to the right of the line is a logo: a square, one-half teal, one-half gray-blue, with an embossed fingerprint printed in metallic copper.*

FINGERPRINT, INC.

DESIGN

PRINT

PROMOTION

920 N. FRANKLIN

CHICAGO, IL 60610

312.266.2850

FAX 312.266.9748

client   Fingerprint, Inc.
design firm   McKnight Kurland Design
           Chicago, Illinois

92

technique   *Envelope flaps and business card backs are printed full bleed gold. Business cards are made to resemble season passes. Fronts are printed full bleed dark metallic gold. At the bottom of business cards, a bar with boxes indicating the days of the week is printed. One day is punched with a hole punch to mimick season pass use.*

client   **Cotter Group**
design firm   **Muller + Company**
               Kansas City, Missouri

technique   *Muted but deep shades of gold, green, purple, or red are used interchangeably in this stationery package. Letterhead backs, envelope insides, and business card fronts are printed full bleed with one of these colors. An "orbital" shape is printed in a darker shade. Business card backs are printed full bleed black with the plant address reversed in white. A partial element from the logo frames the plant address and is printed in the color on the front of the card.*

client   Print NW/Six Sigma
design firm   Hornall Anderson Design Works
                   Seattle, Washington

technique | *A beautiful blue sky is printed full bleed on the back of letterheads and business cards. Sticking up from the bottom of each image are the tops of the World Trade Towers. The consistently-used logo is slightly debossed with silver prism foil.*

client | Odgen Corporation
design firm | McKnight Kurland Design
| Chicago, Illinois

96

technique   *A pattern created from logo elements is printed full bleed on letterhead backs. A lightly screened version of another logo element is printed on letterhead fronts, almost giving the effect of a watermark. Envelope flaps contain the logo, business name and address. The remaining envelope surface contains the full bleed pattern. On envelope fronts, a rectangular section of the pattern is screened giving an easily readable area for an address. Business card fronts and backs are printed with pertinent information. Fronts offer logo, business name, individual's name and title. Backs carry business name, address, motto, phone and fax numbers.*

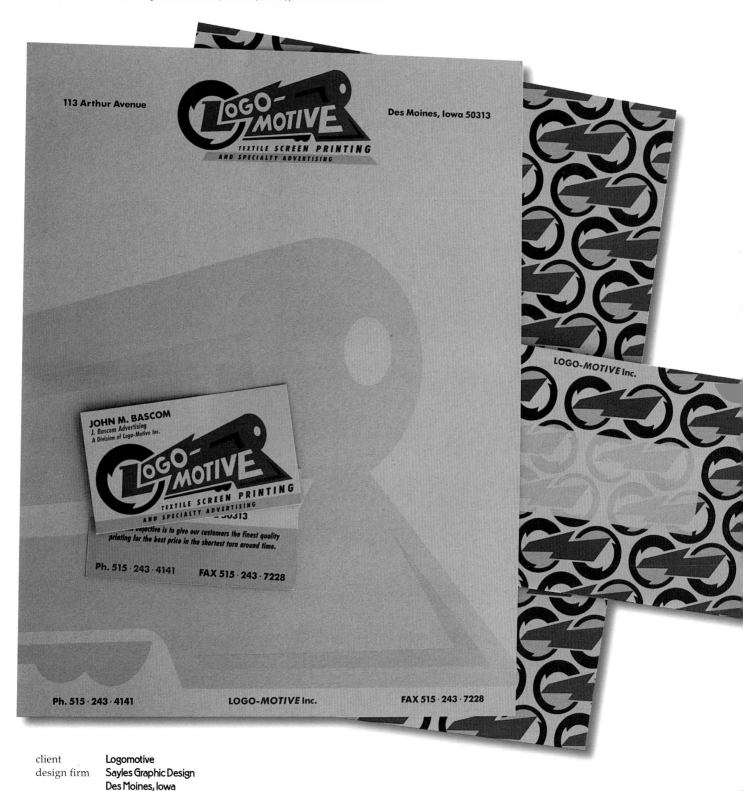

client   **Logomotive**
design firm   **Sayles Graphic Design**
    Des Moines, Iowa

97

technique An interesting die cut is not only aesthetically pleasing but can also be useful. A v-shaped cut at the bottom of the logo gives the image a 35mm-slide look. When letterheads are folded, the cut can be used as a clip to hold the folds together. As this is done, both fronts and backs are shown simultaneously providing a direct relationship between the cranberry-colored full bleed back and the logo's cranberry dot on the front. Envelope flaps are printed with business addresses. Unusual business cards are regular size when received but can be formed into a freestanding column. Printed and then glued together, insides are full bleed cranberry with a reversed white phrase that describes the company. The die cut is positioned on the edge of one of the folds, creating a peephole through which the phrase can be see when the business card is "popped up".

client   Sullivan Pattison Clevenger
design firm   Sullivan Pattison Clevenger
              Portland, Oregon

technique   *Letterheads, envelopes, and business cards of this cutured pearls importers' stationery are blind embossed with two horizontally flowing strands of pearls.*

client   **A&Z PEARLS, INC.**
design firm   **Palko Advertising, Inc.**
                    Lomita, California

technique   *Full bleed green is printed on the backs of letterheads. From the top left corner to the bottom right, a curve is printed in a graduated shade of the green. Letterhead fronts have the mirror image curve, from top right to bottom left, printed in beige. Envelope fronts are printed with a beige curve from top right to bottom left, while flaps are printed full bleed purple with black name and address. Business cards employ the reverse curve technique with black on the back and beige on the front.*

client   Toll-Free Cellular
design firm   Hornall Anderson Design Works
                   Seattle, Washington

technique   *A pinked die cut creates a flat top haircut for the facial logo of this design firm. One-half inch is cut away fron the left side of letterheads leaving one small curve forming an ear for the logo. Envelopes, which include the logo sans hair, are printed and die cut flat. When they are folded and glued, the ear protrudes from the left side. Business cards are pop-ups but can lay flat for filing. When assembled, a bio/mini resume is inside with a touchstone that alerts the viewer to open the card.*

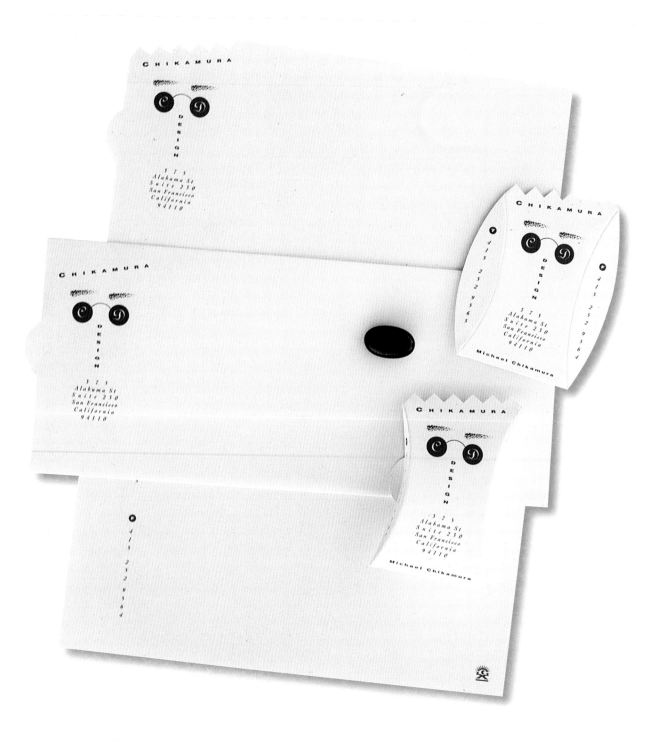

client   Chikamura Design
design firm   Chikamura Design
             San Francisco, California

102

technique   *A unifying theme of this stationery is the die cut leaf. Only the stem end and leaf tip are left attached to paper. Both the leaf vein and stem are blind embossed. Letterheads have the leaf at top center. Custom made envelopes employ it on the flaps which do not use adhesive but have a tab that inserts into another cut on the back. Name cards are standard size when folded. Leaf is on the front. Name, address, and phone number are printed inside.*

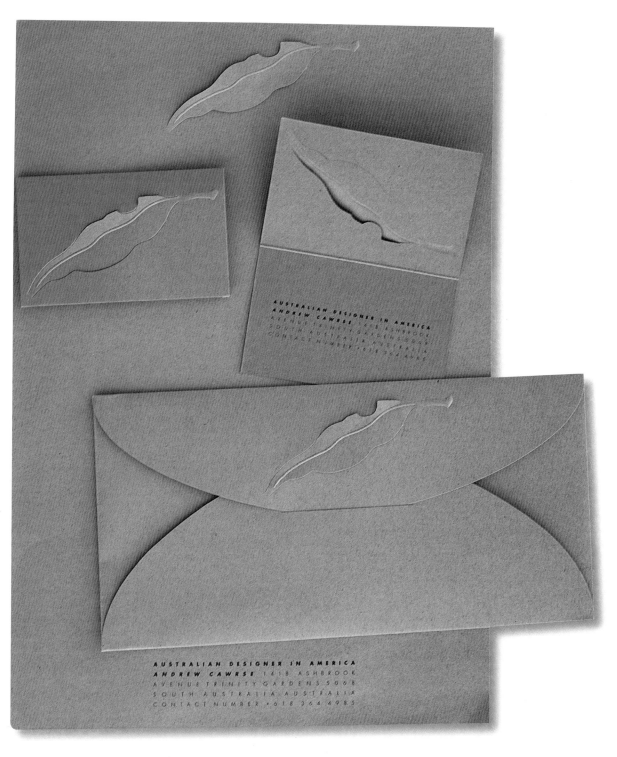

client   Andrew Cawrse (personal stationery)
design firm   Cawrse & Effect
              San Franciso, California

technique   *One of the creative aspects of this package is the use of different angles on paper edges. Letterheads and business cards include only one 90° corner each. Letterhead and business card backs are printed full bleed with a monochromatic texture into which is rendered a geometric shape.*

client   Port Miolla Associates
design firm   Port Miolla Associates
              Norwalk, Connecticut

104

technique   *The logo includes two highly embossed vertical dots inside a "B" which is formed from negative space. Two vertical dots are the letter "B" in braille. The "B" works for both sighted and blind readers, and helps sighted readers understand that blind people read, too.*

client   United States Association of Blind Athletes
design firm   After Hours Creative
              Phoenix, Arizona

technique — *Full bleed maroon is printed on letterhead and business card backs, and envelope insides. The backs of letterheads and business cards also include this photographer's logo, created from a convex lens with opposite "R"s on either side. Name, address and phone are reversed in gold on business card backs. Name and address are printed on envelope flaps.*

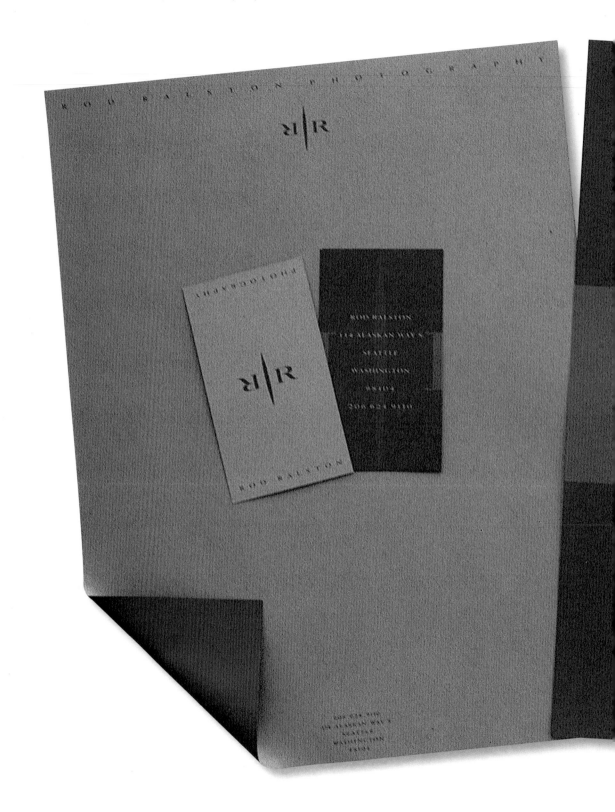

client   Rod Ralston
design firm   Hornall Anderson Design Works
                Seattle, Washington

technique   *A close-up photograph of a coral reef is printed full bleed in monochromatic blue on the letterhead backs of this aqua tanks company. Business cards are on a heavy vellum stock with the coral reef scene printed in metallic blue with a three-sided bleed. Company name is reversed from image.*

client   **Advance Aqua Tanks**
design firm   **Debora Lem Design**
               Torrance, California

technique   *A highly realistic eagle's head is the central portion of this logo. It is blind embossed on letterheads and envelopes.*

client   **Houston Producers Group**
design firm   **Kelman Design Studio**
               Houston, Texas

technique

The gestalt of an orb portion is created with circles used in perspective. Letterheads have this image printed with a four-sided bleed in taupe. Envelope flaps are printed full bleed green with logo dots reversed in white. Business card backs are printed full bleed navy with the orb figure in a lighter blue.

client   Teledesic Corporation
design firm   Hornall Anderson Design Works
              Seattle, Washington

technique   *This designer/educator incorporates facets of both professions into her stationery. Letterheads give usual information in a multiple-choice-quiz format. Manilla envelopes have four die cut holes and address label attached. Business cards define the individual in a dictionary-entry style.*

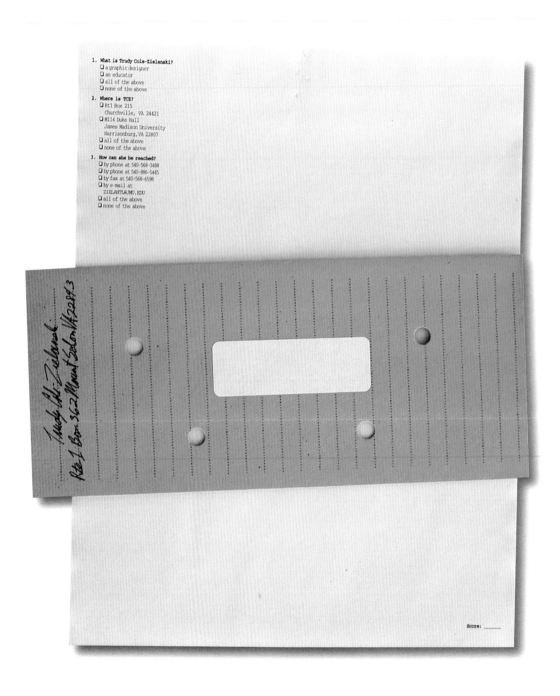

client   **Trudy Cole-Zielanski Design**
design firm   **Trudy Cole-Zielanski Design**
              Harrisonburg and Churchville, VA

technique   *Printing on letterheads and envelopes is slightly*
             debossed. Envelopes include die cut window so that
             address from letterhead shows through. End flaps are
             perforated with a circle die cut to make for easy opening
             and letter removal. Business cards, 4-1/8" x 1-3/8", are
             perforated so logo and information can be separated.

client   **Oh Boy, A Design Company**
design firm   **Oh Boy, A Design Company**
              San Franciso, California

technique   *Letterhead backs are printed in black and gray with*
28 various illustrations of a "brain". These show
through the textured paper to the front of letterheads
imitating a watermark.

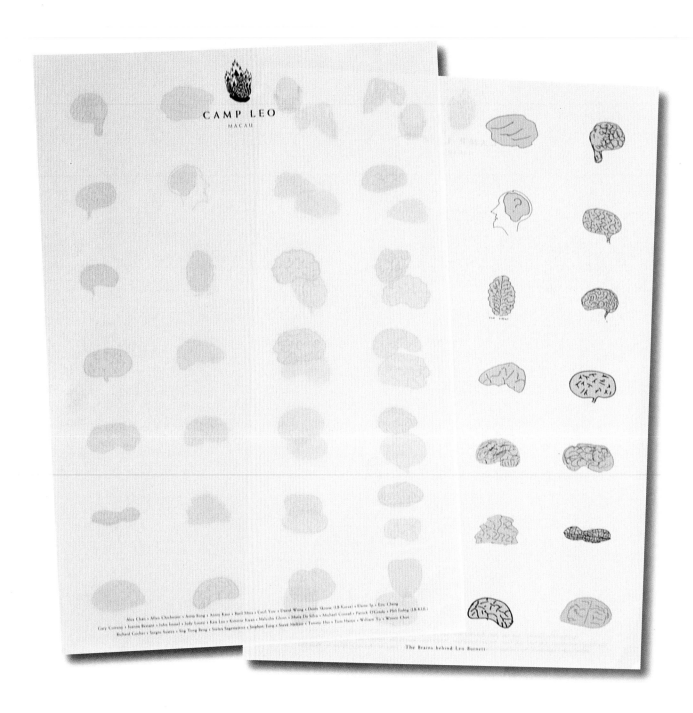

client   **Camp Leo, Leo Burnett**
design firm   **The Design Group**
                 Hong Kong

114

technique   *All printing on letterhead, envelope, and business card*
fronts is slightly embossed. Letterhead backs are printed
full bleed olive green with a small logo at the center
bottom reversed in white. Business cards, which are
extra heavy stock, are printed on the back full bleed with
one of three colors. Logo is reversed in white and
centered on card.

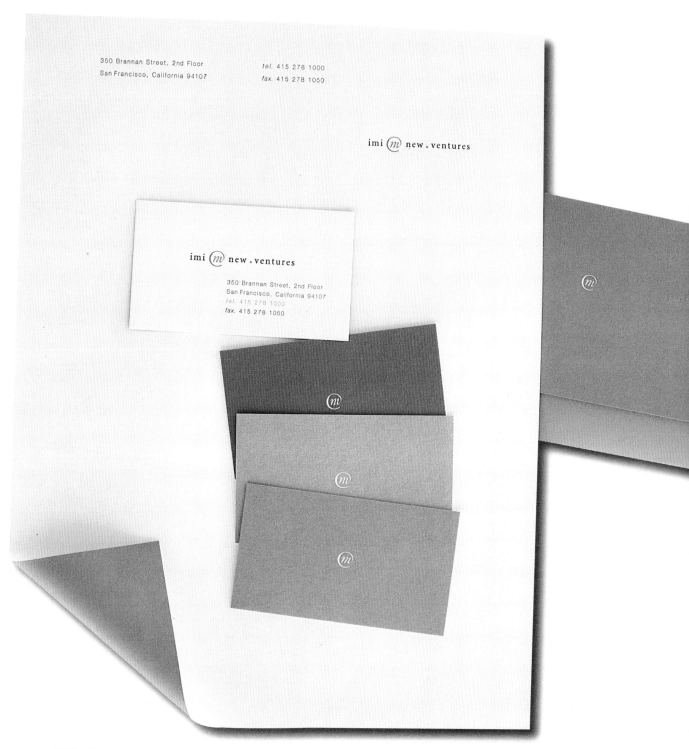

client   **IMI New Ventures**
design firm   **Oh Boy, A Design Company**
               San Franciso, California

technique   *A reiterating phrase reversed from a black bar bleeds from three sides
along the bottom of letterhead, envelope, and business card fronts and
backs. A pattern of blue and yellow cups is created from logo elements
and printed with a two-sided bleed on letterhead front lefts, envelope front
lefts and back rights. Business cards employ the pattern as a full bleed on
the front. Address and numbers are found on business card backs.*

client   Oregon Chai
design firm   Sullivan Pattison Clevenger
              Portland, Oregon

technique   *A photograph of very weathered wood is printed full*
                    bleed on letterhead backs for the Log House Museum.

client   **Southwest Seattle Historical Society**
design firm   **Gable Design Group**
                 Seattle, Washington

118

technique   *A schematic type drawing showing the relationship between circles and squares is part of this company's logo. It is enlarged and printed full bleed on letterhead and business card fronts, and envelope fronts and backs.*

client   **Art Classics Ltd.**
design firm   **Phoenix Creative**
              St. Louis, Missouri

technique   *Iconic imagery is used very effectively in this stationery package. A tiny camera, envelope, or telephone in a rectangular box can be found on an edge of all pieces. Letterhead backs are printed with the telephone/box and "photography for advertising" upside down along the bottom edge. When paper is folded to mail, image and tag line are easily readable to viewer. Envelope insides are printed with a three-sided bleed of celery green. Envelope backs have a geometric, stick figure caricature of a photographer. This is used on letterhead fronts as well. Business cards have on one side the company name, address, phone, and fax. The other side includes the individual's name, title, and specific caricature in the style described above.*

client   **Bruton/ Stroube Photography**
design firm   **Phoenix Creative**
                St. Louis, Missouri

120

technique   *Textured stock is used throughout. The face element of*
the illustrative logo found on letterheads and business
cards is slightly debossed and spot varnished after
printing.

client   **Tracy Sabin Graphic Design**
design firm   **Tracy Sabin Graphic Design**
                San Diego, California

technique   *A black and white collage of clock faces and numbers is printed full bleed on letterhead and business card backs, and envelope insides. A sealing sticker applied to envelope flaps is also printed full bleed with this image. Letterhead and business card backs, and seals have company name and address reversed from collage in white with the exception of a red "A" and "H" in the company name.*

client   **After Hours Creative**
design firm   **After Hours Creative**
                  Phoenix, Arizona

A single dot represents a camera lens or aperature. Business cards have the dot die cut to fulfill the representation even more.

client   Tom Schierlitz
design firm Sagmeister Inc.
            New York, New York

technique   *Logo is embossed on all letterheads, envelopes, and
business cards. The balls within the logo are each
printed a different color: red, yellow, blue. The line at the
logo's bottom is printed black with the word "graphics"
reversed in white.*

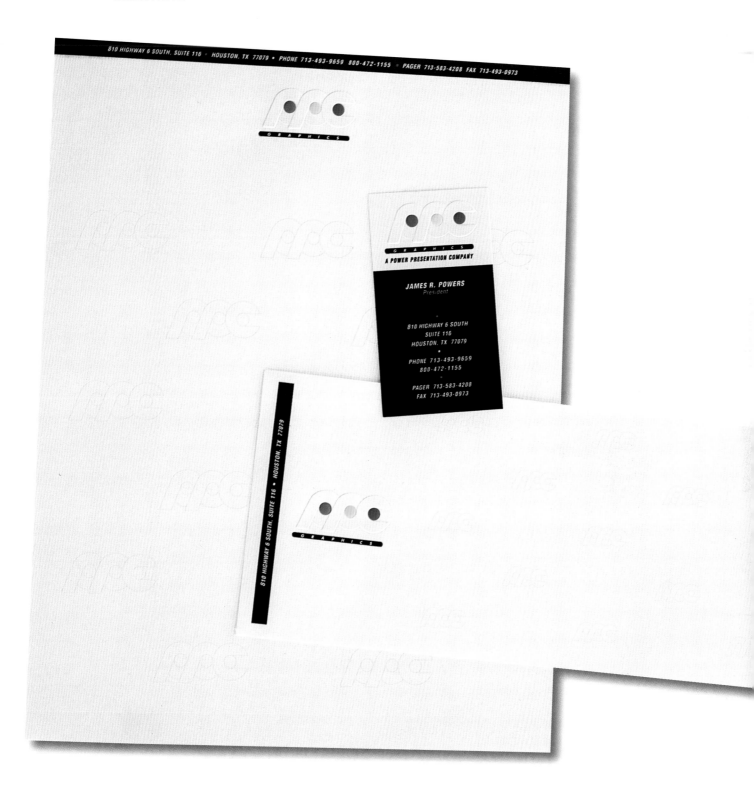

client   PPC Graphics/Power Presentation Company
design firm   Kelman Design Studio
               Houston, Texas

technique   *Logo is embossed and partially printed in gray. Another*
layer of texture is effected by the printing of a scribble
tracing mark pencilled over the logo. The scribble on
letterheads, envelopes and business cards is each
somewhat different.

client   **Congdon Art**
design firm   **Palko Advertising, Inc.**
                Lomita, California

126

technique   *Logo and printing is slightly debossed on letterheads, envelopes, and business cards. Business cards have rounded corners and are extra heavy stock. Presentation folder is blind embossed with logo.*

client   Mires Design Inc.
design firm   Mires Design Inc.
                San Diego, California

technique *An image with a muted-illustrative-tapestry effect is printed full bleed on letterhead and business card backs, and envelope insides. Envelope flaps are printed with a continuation of the image on the front. Envelope flap edges are an unusual, but nice contour.*

TALBOT DESIGN

VISION, TALENT AND A LOT OF RAM

DESIGN GROUP

TE 220 WESTLAKE VILLAGE CA 91362   PH 805.494.0066   FX 805.494.0058

client   Talbot Design Group
design firm   Talbot Design Group
                Westlake Village, California

technique   *A thin strip of paper cut and curled at the top of textured*
              letterheads mimicks a wood shaving for a wood
              craftsman's stationery.

Russ Rogers
Wood Craftsman

Box 1414
Los Gatos
Ca. 95031
408 354 4320

client   **Russ Rogers**
design firm   **J. Robert Faulkner Advertising**
                Venice, California

130

technique   *Logo curve is repeated in letterhead top edges and*
             envelope flaps. A photograph of burlap is printed full
             bleed in green on letterhead backs and envelope flaps.

client   **Designhaus International**
design firm   **Suissa Design**
               Miami Beach, Florida

technique   *A rectangular die cut on folded stock pops up into a*
blind embossed, ribbon tied package for this personal
gift service's stationery. Business card backs are printed
with tagline, name and address.

client   **Consider It Dunn**
design firm   **Cawrse & Effect**
               San Francisco, California

132

technique   *The green, pink and blue used in this package are*
evocative of the art deco buildings of Miami.
Letterhead backs are printed full bleed green. Envelope
insides are printed with a three-sided bleed of pink.
Business card backs are printed full bleed blue.

client   **Coral Gables Dentistry**
design firm   **Goldforest Advertising**
               Miami, Florida

technique   *A starry sky, hill and trees are created in the negative space of this letterheads background by printing with a faint white ink. Backs are printed full bleed navy with a star pattern.*

WILDERNESS
JOURNEYS
Trails to Discovery.

WILDERNESS
JOURNEYS
Trails to Discovery.

1786 Sterling Rd.
Charlotte, NC 28209

1786 Sterling Rd. · Charlotte, North Carolina 28209 · 70

client   Wilderness Journeys
design firm   Sterrett Dymond Advertising
               Charlotte, North Carolina

134

technique   *Earth tones and art nouveau images give a unique feel to this stationery. Each piece contains the cap initials from the name of the firm. "M" is formed in the negative space of the screened artwork printed full bleed on all fronts. A blind embossed, very ornate "E", copper foil seal is attached to each piece to the right and under the name bar. A small black circle has a "D" reversed.*

client   **Mind's Eye Design**
design firm   **Mind's Eye Design**
             New Albany, Indiana

135

technique   *A script capital "R" is blind embossed on letterheads and business cards. Folded business cards have embossing on front and information on the inside. Larger cards are 7-1/4" x 3-3/4" when folded. Card stock printed full bleed with warm metallic pink on both sides offers the base for the die cut script "R" on the front. White paper with basic information is glued inside, showing through the cut on the front.*

client   R. Rega & Associates
design firm   McKnight Kurland Design
           Chicago, Illinois

technique   *Partial logo elements are slightly debossed and foil stamped with silver on textured stock. Enlarged logo continues from envelope fronts to flaps where name and address are also printed.*

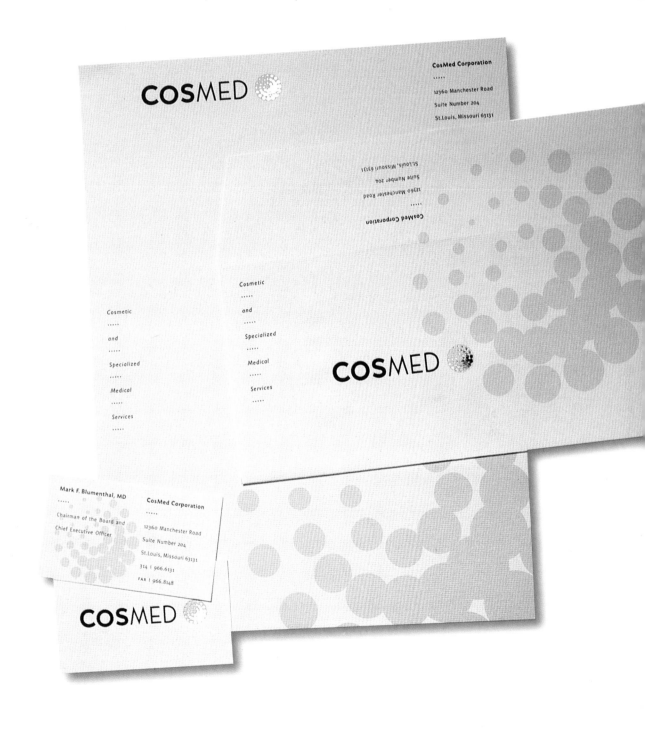

client   **CosMed Corporation**
design firm **Phoenix Creative**
                 St. Louis, Missouri

technique   *The images of a bed, ampersand, and tea pot are*
consistent throughout this bed and breakfast's
stationery. Envelope flaps hold the name, but the
address is printed across envelope back bottoms. Cards
are 3-3/4" x 2". More than just business cards, these are
printed and die cut as luggage check cards. One side is
printed with images, the other has printed lines
between name and address for notes, messages,
reservation times.

client   **Ruta Bagage**
design firm   **Paprika**
          Montréal, Québec

138

technique   *The word "loop" is rendered in three-dimensional objects, blind embossed and printed in shades of gray on all stationery pieces.*

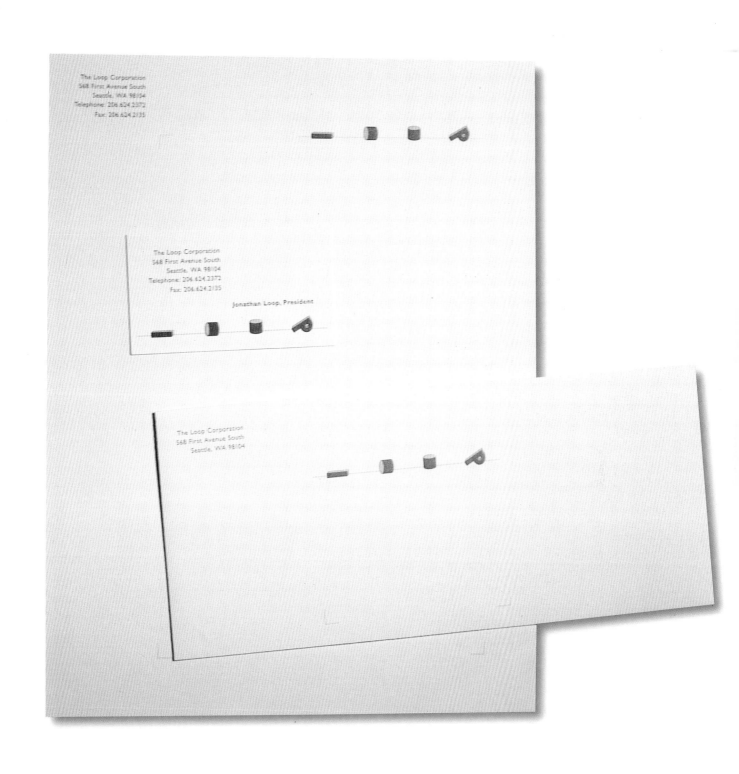

client   **The Loop Corporation**
design firm **Hansen Design Company**
               Seattle, Washington

technique *Black is printed full bleed on letterhead and business card backs, and envelopes insides. Reversed in small letters, in the center of each, are verbs that define this firm. A rather vague but visually interesting collage is printed full bleed in very light tan on letterhead and business card fronts, and envelope fronts and backs.*

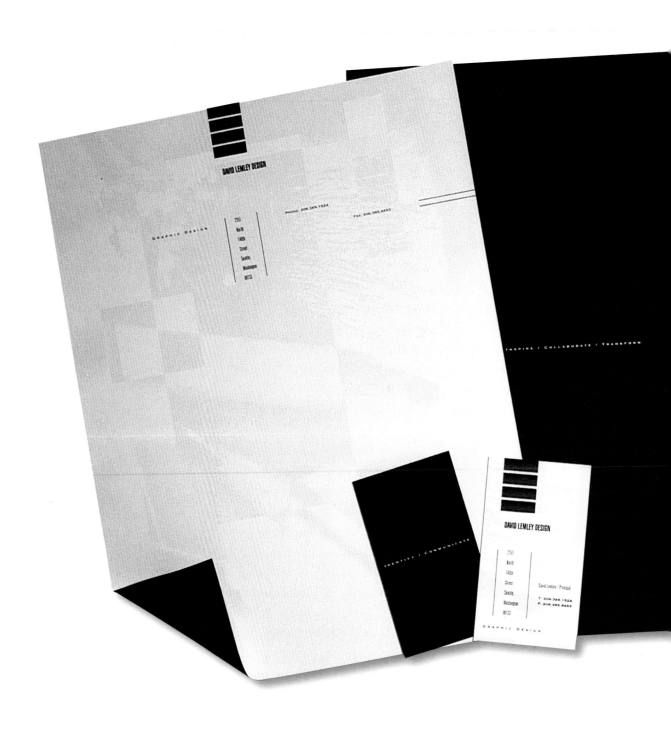

David Lemley Design
David Lemley Design
Seattle, Washington

DAVID LEMLEY DESIGN

GRAPHIC DESIGN

2151
North
140th
Street
Seattle,
Washington
98133

technique   *Angles of letterhead and business card edges add
distinction to this stationery package. Envelopes are
printed with a three-sided bleed of an aqua bar on front
lefts and back rights. Name and address are on
envelope flaps. Business cards have logo on the front
and other information on the back.*

client   **Von Tress Architects**
design firm   **Phoenix Creative**
               St. Louis, Missouri

technique   *Artwork reminiscent of the height of railroad luxury travel is utilized well. Full-size envelope flaps are printed with art and tag line.*

client   Grand Central Post
design firm Phoenix Creative
             St. Louis, Missouri

technique   *Peephole die cuts on envelope flaps and business card fronts reveal logo beneath. The short cut front on folded business cards allows individual's name to show along with logo. Open to reveal address and numbers.*

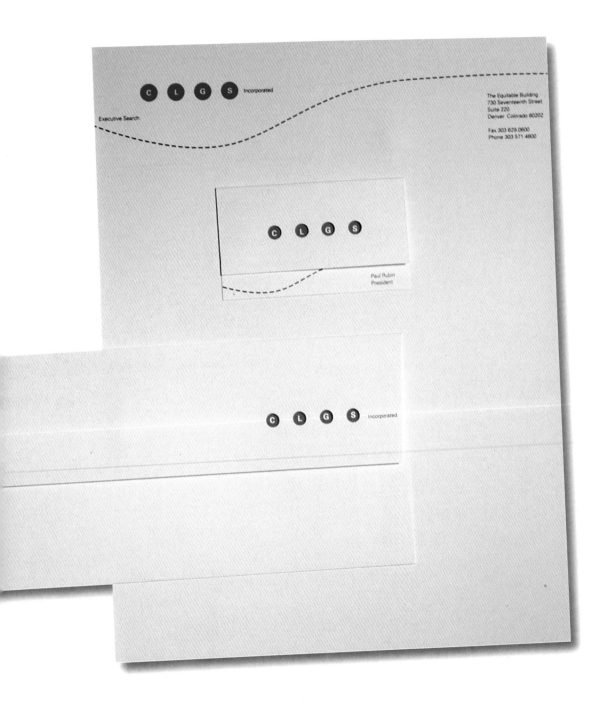

client   **CLGS Incorporated**
design firm   **Ema Design Inc.**
           Denver, Colorado

technique   *Curves. Letterhead front right edges are curved. Envelope flaps are curved. Business cards are ovals. Phone index card top edges are curved. Letterhead backs are printed full bleed yellow. Envelope insides are printed with red. The logo on envelope fronts bleeds off left side and wraps around to envelope backs. Name and address is printed on envelope flaps parallel with the curved edge. The oval logo is the business card on one side; name, address, numbers on flip side. Phone index cards are printed full bleed yellow on front, full bleed red on back.*

client   Lambert Design
design firm   Lambert Design
              Dallas, Texas

technique	*Business cards have logo enlarged and printed full bleed on back.*
client	**Innovative Futures**
design firm	**Becker Design** **Milwaukee, Wisconsin**

technique	*Slightly textured, oval business cards are printed full bleed black on back. This repeats the logo image which is on front with other information.*
client	**Chris McPherson Photography**
design firm	**Graphics 2** **Scottsdale, Arizona**

technique	*These business cards are normal size when folded, but when opened a die cut along the fold creates a pop-up bar which is printed in two colors with a reversed tag line.*
client	**Barrett Communications**
design firm	**Barrett Communications** **Cambridge, Massachusetts**

146

technique   *Logos are slightly debossed, printed in black, and spot varnished on all pieces. Letterheads and business cards carry the logo at the top. The top halves of these logos have been die cut giving a gear effect.*

client   **Die Works**
design firm   **Webster Design Associates**
              Omaha, Nebraska

technique   *Natural elements are formed into a photographic collage and printed with different intensities on letterhead borders, envelope insides, and on one side of business cards with a full bleed. Letterhead backs, envelope flaps, and other side of business cards are printed full bleed red. Logo is on red side of business cards, information on nature side.*

client   **Clark and Company**
design firm   **Clark and Company**
              Phoenix, Arizona

148

technique   *An all-over hands pattern is reversed from muted tones on letterhead fronts, envelope fronts and flaps. A large star is used as a different letterhead background printed in muted colors. Envelope backs are printed full bleed in package colors. Folded business cards have a wavy die cut opening edge. Inside is information while back is printed full bleed with hands pattern.*

client   **Community Partnership**
design firm   **Gee + Chung**
    San Francisco, California

technique *Scallops are die cut along letterhead bottoms, envelope flaps, and opposite edges of business cards. Antique style images prevail throughout. Letterhead fronts are printed light green, with a bright green and black female head. Letterhead backs are printed scarlet with a woman's arm in scarlet and white. Envelope insides are printed scarlet with a scarlet and white button-up shoe. Business cards, 3-1/2" x 2-1/4" when folded, contain two die cut holes in the center, through which a black satin ribbon is threaded and tied in a bow. Fronts are bright green with female head. Backs are black with white and green type. Insides are scarlet with a scarlet and white camera and lipstick. All pieces have strikingly white borders.*

client   Lou Freeman Photography
design firm   **Big Design Group**
            Atlanta, Georgia

150

technique   *The gold from the logo is printed full bleed on letterhead,*
              envelope, and business card backs. Envelope and
              business card backs also include part of the logo, name,
              and address in black.

client   **Spangler Design Team**
design firm   **Spangler Design Team**
              Minneapolis, Minnesota

technique   *A series of colored bars aids in the definition of this stationery's design. The bottoms of letterheads and business cards are cut at an angle so that the bottom bar bleeds off the page.*

client   **Stewart Monderer Design, Inc.**
design firm   **Stewart Monderer Design, Inc.**
                Boston, Massachusetts

152

technique   *Repetition of "D" contributes to unity in this package. Die cut circles and address line each form an abstract "D" on letterheads and envelopes. A small capital "D" is embossed and printed in black. Both bleeding off the bottom of the page, "design" is blind embossed across a large "D" printed in metallic silver. Metallic silver is printed full bleed on fronts and backs of envelopes. Fronts are blind embossed with small "D" at top; "Dawson" across both the bottom and over a large, black "D". One edge of envelope flaps is curved, mimicking "D". Business cards are uniquely sized at 4" x 1-3/4". Fronts are printed full bleed silver, blind embossed with a small capital "D", bleed a large, black "D" off the bottom, and include the company name and die cut circles each in the form of an abstract "D". Backs are printed full bleed black with individual's name and address reversed in white. "Design" is blind embossed and bleeds from two sides.*

client   **Dawson Design Associates, Ltd.**
design firm   **Rowley Associates**
                Scottsdale, Arizona

153

technique
A pattern of descriptive computer phrases is printed full bleed violet on letterhead backs and with a three-sided bleed inside business cards. Envelope flaps are printed full bleed metallic gold with fine violet lines; envelope backs are printed full bleed violet. Envelope flaps and back top edges are cut on an ascending angle. Side edges of business cards are likewise unusually angled. Fronts include cubistic logo. Inside is information. Backs are printed full bleed metallic gold with a violet circle containing previously noted phrasing.

154

client   Xinet, Inc.
design firm   Gee + Chung Design
San Franciso, California

technique   *Printed in blocks of different colors, a bar is formed and bleeds from the right edge of letterheads and left edge of envelopes. Within one of the solid color blocks is the blind embossed logo. Second sheets of letterheads include the same embossing, but no printing. Envelope backs are printed with a green bar with address reversed.*

client   Polivka Logan Design, Inc.
design firm   Polivka Logan Design, Inc.
          Minneapolis, Minnesota

technique   *Kinetic scribbling is printed full bleed green on letterhead backs and envelope insides. While folded business cards have name, address, and numbers on fronts, they incorporate the scribbling on backs and one-half of insides. This leaves space for messages if need be.*

client   **Michael Braden**
design firm   **Hansen Design Company**
               Seattle, Washington

technique   *A border of black and purple blocks bleeds off opposite edges of letterhead fronts, sealing edge of envelope flaps, and opposite edges of business card fronts and backs. Letterhead backs are printed full bleed purple which still allows the paper's visible texture to show through. One side of 3-1/2" x 2-3/16" business card is printed with business name and artwork, the other offers information.*

client   Studio A
design firm   Deep Design
                Atlanta, Georgia

158

technique   *Embossed and printed with plum and metallic copper, the logo is on all pieces. Letterhead backs and envelope flaps are printed full bleed plum with a line-and-circle version of company name in copper and cream. Envelope backs are printed with a descriptive tag line. Business cards are average size when folded and possess an interesting series of die cuts on the front. Insides carry all information while backs are printed full bleed plum with a striped pattern of metallic copper.*

client   **Berman Marketing**
design firm   **Gee + Chung Design**
              San Francisco, California

technique   *Interesting levels of dimension, are created with
transparent elements which are debossed and printed
in this logo.*

C U R R E N T   C O M M U N I C A T I O N S

1048 Irvine Avenue, Suite 612, Newport Beach, CA 92660, Ph: 714.646.5768 Fx: 714.646.6915

client   **Current Communications**
design firm   **Tracy Sabin Graphic Design**
              San Diego, California

160

technique   *Cream yellow is printed with a three-sided bleed on letterhead, envelope, and business card fronts. The mirror image is printed on all backs. Envelope flaps carry name and address. Business card fronts have the logo, and backs offer all other information.*

client   **Metaphase Design Group**
design firm   **Phoenix Creative**
               St. Louis, Missouri

technique   *Deep shades are printed full bleed on the backs of*
             letterheads. Information side of business cards have a
             border of rusty red which bleeds off four sides. The other
             side is simply printed with the "think deep" icon, one of
             four used throughout the package.

client   **Deep Design**
design firm   **Deep Design**
               Atlanta, Georgia

162

technique   *Nature silhouette images are printed in an all-over*
pattern on the textured stock of the backs of letterheads,
and fronts and backs of envelopes.

client   **Amazon University**
design firm   **Savage Design Group**
                  Houston, Texas

technique   *Photographs of old, some antique, objects clues in the viewer as to what types of things are sold by this business. Letterhead fronts picture six objects while second sheet and business card backs are printed with a random collage of objects reversed from dark gray. Purple envelopes are printed with collage on front in gold. Envelope flaps have one object, description of items and address. Front of folded business cards includes business name and logo. Inside is opened for other information.*

client   **Creatures of Habit**
design firm   **Fire House, Inc.**
                  Evansville, Indiana

technique   *Very fibrous stock adds visual texture to this stationery. Logo is slightly debossed, printed in purple, and spot varnished. Envelope flaps are printed with name and address.*

BROOKS**HOWARD**

11815 Addison St
North Hollywood
California 91607

telephone
(818) 506.1209
fax
(818) 985.8722

Compact Discs
Laser Discs
CD ROM
Audio Cassettes
Video
Packaging and Printing

client   Brooks Howard
design firm   Evenson Design Group
                Culver City, California

technique   *Logo adds its own dimension as it casts a screened*
              shadow. Letterhead and business card top edges are
              die cut along a black bar bleed.

client   **The Bowyer Studio**
design firm   **O'Keefe Marketing**
                Richmond, Virginia

166

technique   *Textured paper is used for all stationery pieces. An*
            enlarged graduated version of the logo is printed full bleed
            in cream yellow on letterhead and envelope fronts.
            Business card backs are printed with the same image in
            full bleed blue. Envelope backs and flaps are printed
            with full bleed yellow.

client   **Fox 25 Boston**
design firm   **Fox 25 Design Department**
                Dedham, Massachusetts

technique   *Logo is blind embossed in such a manner that negative space creates identical elements as that which is embossed. Logo is embossed on letterheads and business cards. All stationery pieces use textured paper.*

client   **Contact, Inc.**
design firm   **Graphics 2**
             Scottsdale, Arizona

technique   *This clean logo treatment is the same for all pieces. Large logo element is blind embossed. Remaining logo is printed.*

client   **Graphics 2**
design firm   **Graphics 2**
              Scottsdale, Arizona

technique   *The logo is created with an upright "I" and a skewed "A"
which acts as a shadow. Logo is slightly debossed. "I" is
printed black and spot varnished. "A" is copper foil
stamped. Indigo is printed full bleed on letterhead and
business card backs. Hunter green is printed with a
three-sided bleed inside envelopes. Business card fronts
are printed with logo. Backs have information in
reversed white type.*

client   Image Alchemy
design firm   Shaun Hubbard Graphic Designer
                Seattle, Washington

170

technique   *Blurs behind the logo create effective shadowing for a feeling of depth. The corners of letterheads and business cards are die cut with an inverted curve. Website is printed on envelope flaps. Business cards are of heavy stock and are 3-1/2" x 1-3/4". Printed on both sides, one side of business card contains logo, business name, individual's name, address and numbers, the other is printed with logo and business name only.*

client   Virtual Vineyards, Inc.
design firm   Gee + Chung Design
                San Francisco, California

technique *Pet-name-tag logo is embossed and silver foil stamped.*
Name on tag is debossed and printed in black. S-hook
in tag is slightly debossed and silver foil stamped.
Letterheads incorporate name tag into a choker chain
that runs horizontally and bleeds off two edges.
Envelopes and business cards use the logo with a
horizontally-running collar which bleeds off two edges.
Envelopes have collar printed on fronts and backs.

client **Pet Fair Productions**
design firm **Jamie Sheehan Design**
Seattle, Washington

technique   *A pale green swiss dot pattern is printed full bleed on letterhead fronts and backs; full bleed on envelope fronts, backs and insides; with a three-sided bleed on one side of business cards. A pattern made with the letters of "Bandilu e" is printed across the bottoms of letterhead fronts and envelope flaps in pale green, and on one side of business cards in vivid colors with a full bleed.*

client   **Bandilu Entertainment**
design firm   **Melanie Paykos Design**
              Culver City, California

technique   *Strong primary colors relate the pieces of this stationery package. Letterhead backs are printed full bleed red, with Board Members' names reversed in white and backwards. They can be read easily from the front if a light source is behind the paper. Second sheets are printed full bleed yellow. Business card backs are printed full bleed blue.*

client   VCU Ad Center
design firm   O'Keefe Marketing
                Richmond, VA

174

technique   *A cube is formed by blind embossed dots and arrowheads on letterhead tops, envelope flaps, and business cards. Business cards are printed on one side full bleed royal blue with company name and address reversed in white. Turn it over for the individual's name in gray.*

client   **Technology Vision Group**
design firm   **Russell Leong Design**
    Palo Alto, California

technique   *Gotcha! This package doesn't contain embossing,*
printing on the back, die cuts, or any special texturing.
The printing of the photograph of the paper clip does,
however, add dimension to the stationery. The bend of
the steel and shadow behind it give it special effect and
certainly add equivalent interest as any of the
aforementioned processes.

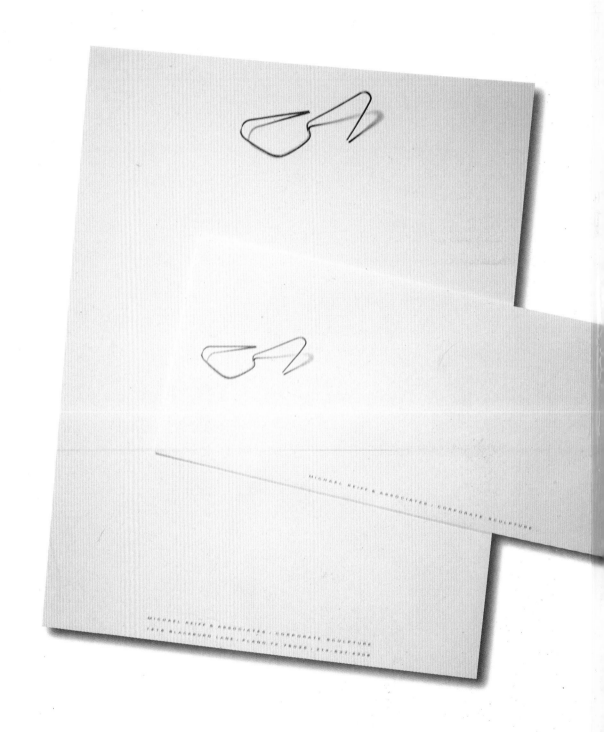

client   **Michael Reiff & Associates**
design firm   **Goldsmith/Jeffrey, Inc.**
New York, New York

176

David E. Carter has produced more books on logo design and corporate identity than anyone else in the world.

How many? "Oh, somewhere between fifty and sixty," Carter says. (His 9th grade math teacher once told him, "you're not college material.")

Undaunted, Carter graduated from the University of Kentucky, and received a master's degree from the Ohio University School of Journalism. He recently received an MBA degree from Syracuse University, and will soon graduate from the Harvard Business School's 3-year management program for company owners/presidents (OPM).

Somewhere in between all this, Carter founded a national advertising agency which quickly won a Clio Award; started a TV production company that did work for PBS and *The Johnny Carson Show* and won seven Emmy Awards; and he still does corporate identity consulting for major clients, primarily in Indonesia and Thailand.

His greatest accomplishment, however, has nothing to do with business. "No matter how successful you are," he says, "if your kids don't turn out right, nothing else really counts. My two daughters have grown up to be terrific adults."

He and his wife live in Kentucky and Florida.

ISBN 0-8230-2753-8